MAKING FRIENDS
written and illustrated by
Andrew Matthews

From Mama
use it in good
health.

PRICE STERN SLOAN
Los Angeles

Making Friends

Published by Price Stern Sloan, Inc.
11150 Olympic Boulevard, Suite 650
Los Angeles, California 90064
Printed in Singapore by Grenadier Press.
1 0 9 8 7 6 5 4 3 2

Also by the same author: **BEING HAPPY!**

This book has been printed on acid-free paper.

ISBN 0-8431-2969-7

PREFACE

Human relationships are the source of most of life's pleasure and pain. This book shares some ideas and strategies which can give you more pleasure and less pain !

You may have had the occasional thought about an acquaintance . . .

"It's impossible not to argue with that person" or "I don't know how to talk to this woman!" There are options for dealing with these people that you may not have tried, and we'll take a look at these.

We always have choices in how we deal with others, but most of us lapse into familiar ruts and patterns.

You will know some people who seem to be able to talk to anybody. They meet someone in a restaurant and you automatically figure that they have been lifelong buddies. You say, "How long have you known each other?" and they say, "We've never met before."

These unique individuals are not born lucky — they simply use skills, they have a particular awareness, and it can be developed.

Certain things are no fun to do alone.

Have you ever tried having a party by yourself?

Things like watching movies, eating dinner, playing cards, driving to work, fixing problems, planning vacations — and going on them — things like moving house, making plans . . . and having parties, need company — the people you care about.

A joyous life is one filled with friendships. Imagine losing your job, or your money, or your fancy car . . . No doubt you'd survive. But losing your closest friends, is a different matter.

Our happiness hinges on attitude — our attitude toward ourselves, work, effort, goals, our response to failure, disappointment, pleasure, pain and the whole life puzzle. My first book, **Being Happy!** is about such things. I call it a gentle philosophy of life.

There is, however, a key variable in the happiness equation — OTHER PEOPLE.

This book is about THE OTHERS. Those "others" with whom we laugh, hurt, shout, swear, cry, try, work, play, plan, debate . . . those whom we love, trust, tolerate, blame, believe, and occasionally avoid.

That's why this book, **Making Friends**.

There are no simple formulae for making friends. Certainly it takes more than a healthy self-esteem and good table manners to earn the trust of others. There's a balance between give and take, between duty to oneself and to others. And then there's generosity, sensitivity, good humor, a little wisdom.

Our world is made of layers. We have the inside world – friends and family; the outside world – bosses and bank managers; and the occasional extra-terrestrial – salesmen at the door and . . .

Different people require different treatment. (You don't treat your boss like you treat your wife.) Nevertheless, we seek a tranquil co-existence with people from all layers.

Everything is always up for review – companies analyze returns and change their strategies accordingly. We should do the same (with ourselves). Take stock. Ask ourselves: what am I doing and is it enriching my life?

Take Fred, who has all the trendy gear. Armani shirt, Cardin suit, Gucci shoes, and a concertina of credit cards. He's got a gold watch on his arm and a matching Porsche in the garage. And he might argue that he's doing everything "right". But Fred might want to ask himself, "If I'm doing all the right things, where are my real friends? How is it that Barry in his battered old Toyota is getting all the laughs and scoring with the ladies?"

Like Fred, we can benefit by asking ourselves some relevant questions, like . . . " Am I reliable? Do I feel superior? Do I feel inferior? Am I running scared? Do I take myself too seriously? Can I laugh at myself? Do I listen? Am I responsible? Am I a fun person to be around, or do I bore everyone to death?

The first lesson of friendship is: IF YOU WANT FRIENDSHIP, YOU MUST BE A FRIEND FIRST.

Andrew Matthews
August, 1990

CONTENTS

YOU AND OTHERS

It's no good being someone's "other half" — you're a whole person.

WE ALL GET NERVOUS!

Most people are more scared than you are.

Have you ever been scared of someone? If it is any consolation, many people who look cool, calm, collected and oozing with confidence are scared stiff.

You spot a glamorous lady sitting by herself at a party, casually sipping her martini. You think to yourself, "She looks very calm and self assured." But if you could read her thoughts you might be amazed... "Are people wondering why I'm by myself?... If I'm attractive, why don't I have a man?... My breasts are too small... I wish I was as smart as my sister... I want to go to the bathroom but everyone will look at me ...If that guy comes over and talks to me, I'll die!..."

We look at the business tycoon and say, "He's got it made!" He looks at himself and worries about his paunch and his red nose, wonders why

he can't talk to his kids and agonizes about whether he's losing his touch, his hair and his money.

Isn't life a big joke? We look at others and figure that they have got it all together. They look at us and figure we have got it all together. We live in fear of other people who themselves live in fear of us.

For a number of years I conducted a seminar at the beginning of which participants were required to introduce themselves. At those seminars I would have doctors, teachers, grandmothers, models, salespeople, teenagers and business executives panicking and perspiring at the thought of having to speak for thirty seconds before a roomful of people. And the reason behind their fear – "OTHER PEOPLE MIGHT THINK I'M NOT GOOD ENOUGH."

We should remember that everyone has "I'm not good enough" thoughts. Nobody has it all together.

Apart from anxiety, fearing each other leads to misunderstandings. You may have had the experience where you had some neighbors who never talked to you, so you didn't talk to them. You concluded that they were unfriendly snobs. Whenever you passed in the street, they'd be studying the clouds and you'd look at the cracks in the pavement.

Then finally after a year or two, you were introduced to each other and you became immediate friends. You were frightened to say "Hello", and figured THEY had a problem. They were scared to say "Hello", and reasoned that YOU had a problem.

Few people have the confidence they appear to have. You may look fairly harmless to yourself when you brush your teeth at the bathroom mirror, but don't be fooled. YOU'RE SCARY. You make lots of people nervous. So if you've spent sleepless nights in fear of others, give yourself permission to stop it. And whenever you are tempted to write off others as being opinionated and stuck up, give them the benefit of the doubt. Chances are they're scared.

IN A NUTSHELL

Thoreau wrote, "Most people live lives of quiet desperation." We each have our insecurities. Refuse to live in fear of a bunch of people who may, like you, be quietly desperate!

HABITS

Have you ever noticed that when someone has an irritating habit, he or she is usually the last to know? It is the person with the foul mouth who has no idea that he is turning people off. It is the fellow who lives on garlic sausages who never finds out that he smells like one.

What does that suggest to us about our own irritating habits? We are usually the LAST to know.

I have a friend who talks and talks and talks. Having a conversation with her is like standing in front of a machine gun. She is very intelligent and highly educated, but she doesn't realize how she affects people. She is notorious for her one-way conversations. She has been told more than once of her problem, but somehow she has never absorbed the message. She is socially handicapped and doesn't know it.

We need to be aware of how we affect others, and be prepared to do something about it. An excuse like, "That's just the way I am" is an expensive way to live a life. If several people tell us that we talk too much or that we're always late or that we preach, or have bad manners, we can profit from that information. It is usually a sign that we have a problem.

One way to improve your self awareness is to talk to a friend you really trust. Find people whom you know will not deliberately berate you, and ask them, "How do I come across?" Let them know that you are interested in improving yourself and have them understand that you want their total honesty.

Some questions you may like to start with –

"Do I talk too much?"

"Do I complain too much?"

"Do I drink too much?"

"Does my breath smell?"

"Is my language offensive?"

"Do I talk too much about my health, my partner, my insomnia, money, religion, jogging etc."

"How are my table manners?"

"Do I eat with my mouth open?"

"Am I ever boring?"

"Are there any clothes in my wardrobe that should be in the garbage?"

These are personal questions, but you've got to know! Whatever your friend tells you, don't take it as gospel, but give the ideas due consideration. Ask yourself, "Have other people ever told me the same thing?" Ask yourself "If I was living/working with me, how would I like it?"

It may be that you do offend other people and decide not to change. That is OK, so long as you know what is happening and what your behavior may be costing you.

Some people have the attitude, "I just have one problem – and it's with the five billion other people in the world. I'm perfect, but they don't understand me . . ."

Ideally, others will be tolerant of your weaknesses, but you can't always count on it. While you may choose to exercise tolerance yourself, lots of people don't! Many an aspiring executive has been overlooked for a promotion because he dressed like a slob. Many a marriage has ended on the rocks because the wife talked incessantly or the husband never listened.

IN A NUTSHELL

Outstanding individuals develop a special self awareness which endears them to others. To influence others positively, we need to develop that kind of awareness.

COMPARING OURSELVES

"LEARNING TO LOVE YOURSELF IS THE GREATEST LOVE OF ALL."

You have to love yourself before you can love anyone else. You have to believe that if you want to improve your lot. Books and seminars on personal growth also preach the same message.
WHEN WE ARE OVER CRITICAL OF OURSELVES, WE TEND TO RESENT PEOPLE WHO ARE DOING BETTER. Take Frank who is married to Jane. Frank is an upwardly mobile executive. Jane stays at home with the kids. She feels she leads a dull life while Frank is carving out a career. Result – Jane resents Frank. Day and night she criticizes the man whom she swore to love and cherish in sickness and in health. And the reason – Jane doesn't like herself, so she finds things wrong with Frank – and everyone else.

When others do well, Jane feels inadequate, so she gets critical. Her criticism really has nothing to do with Frank – it has to do with her own self-concept. Their relationship can never improve until she starts to like herself better.

IF WE SEE ONLY **OUR** FAULTS, WE EXPECT THAT OTHERS WILL SEE ONLY **OUR** FAULTS. Therefore, the unfortunate fact is, we're always waiting to be rejected . . .

Take Fred who believes he's a failure. He worries that his girlfriend, Mary, might also think he's a failure. He is very sensitive about not being

as successful as the neighbors. He knows he's overweight and suspects his nose is too big. Because Fred doesn't like himself, he feels self-conscious and second rate. He fears that Mary is on the lookout for someone better. He is easily offended and he nags her daily. Poor Fred can't forget his own problems for long enough to really care for Mary. Result – Mary feels unloved because Fred feels bad about himself. When our self-image is poor, our friends always suffer.

COMPARING OURSELVES IS A TRAP. There will always be people who are more talented, richer, smarter, wittier or more popular than we are. Parents and teachers and lovers may often say, "Why can't you be more like your brother?" The answer is, "Because I'm NOT my brother. If I were, I'd be exactly like him!"

At some point we each must decide, "I'm a unique individual. I don't have to be a carbon copy of my mother or my neighbor or anybody else." We can affirm, "I'm not perfect but I'm doing the best I can with the information available. I'm working at being a better person AND I accept myself for the moment."

We, like Jane and Fred, need to stop measuring ourselves against our friends or partners or the Joneses across the street. Instead, we begin to set ourselves goals and targets which make sense to us. We measure our growth this year in terms of our OWN progress last year, rather than against the neighbors' progress. We draw our satisfaction and sense of worth from our own development.

In Jane's case, she has lots of options to improve the way she feels about herself, and in the process become a better companion. Instead of criticising Frank, she can set herself meaningful, and achievable goals at home, for future employment, for her continuing education, for shedding excess weight, for her leisure time. She'll soon figure out that YOU DON'T GET OUT OF A HOLE BY PULLING OTHERS INTO IT. You have to climb out.

Similarly, Fred needs to make a concerted effort. Make the transition from "comparing" himself to improving himself — building on his minor successes, supporting Mary where possible, concentrating on his own good points while accepting his lesser attributes — like his well-developed nose.

When we cease continually comparing ourselves, we free ourselves to appreciate (and compliment) others. We then quit the mental point scoring . . . "she's got that fancy jacket, extra degree, new trophy/boyfriend — does that mean she's better than I?" We scrap the destructive "IF YOU'RE MORE, I'M LESS" notion.

Loving yourself is not a matter of boasting to all the world. It is a matter of self acceptance — of noting your qualities as well as your shortcomings. To enjoy fruitful relationships, YOU HAVE TO CHOOSE TO BE YOUR OWN BEST FRIEND.

Fred says, "I'm still not convinced that I should like myself." Well, there's another very simple reason why Fred must like himself first. IF HE DOESN'T LIKE HIMSELF, HE WON'T BELIEVE THAT ANYONE ELSE WOULD LIKE HIM! This leads to more problems —

• When people are friendly with Fred, he may decide a) they want something or b) there must be something drastically wrong with them that they should want his company

• If he continually criticizes himself, all his friends may decide he has a problem — and avoid Fred altogether

• Fred may also fear that nobody could possibly like him if they got to know him really well — so he may subconsciously destroy his relationships before others have a chance to reject him.

The psychoanalysts, Bernard Berkowitz and Mildred Newman, write — "People who do not love themselves can adore others, because adoration is making someone else big and ourselves small. They can desire others, because desire comes out of a sense of inner incompleteness, which demands to be filled. But they cannot love others, because love is an affirmation of the living, growing being in all of us. If you don't have it, you can't give it."

CHOOSING TO SUFFER

If our self-image is very poor, we may choose to make our life miserable to punish ourselves. Suffering, like any behavior, has its payoffs . . .

• If you've always suffered, there is a certain security in suffering. You understand it and besides, change is frightening. It's a little like illness, where people will sometimes admit, "If I ever got well, I would have no excuses any more. It's kind of convenient being sick."

• We may also reason that failure will somehow make us loveable . . "Perhaps if I continue to suffer long enough, my parents or my partner or somebody will feel sorry for me and start to love me." Unfortunately, healthy relationships aren't founded on pity.

• We may keep suffering, waiting for God to notice how miserable we are – hoping that one day He'll lose his patience and say, "That's it! I can't stand watching you mess up any more." And then He'll fix everything for us.

As our self-image improves, suffering ceases to be an acceptable alternative, but some of us do choose it, and it's our perfect right to do so.

HOW CAN I LIKE MYSELF?

You say, "Well, I agree now that it is important to iove – or at least like myself – but how do I do it if I feel a failure? What if I've been put down by my parents and ridiculed by my teachers, and what if I hate my piggy eyes and my crooked teeth?"

Well, it's possible to come to accept yourself and even love yourself as you are. It might be a long term job, but the stakes are high. Your whole happiness hangs on how you feel about you. The success of all your friendships depends on you accepting you.

Ask yourself, "Do I want to lift myself up or pull myself down?"

First, it helps to review how you got your self-image.

WHO DO YOU THINK YOU ARE?

The earliest feedback you got came from your family, and most of it was NEGATIVE..."Don't make a mess...you're ALWAYS breaking things ...you NEVER do what you're told... you're driving me nuts... don't be so STUPID... I could murder you children..." Some parents manage to balance the negatives with positives, but for many kids it seems a one-way street. Oh, our parents loved us, but so often life just got in the way. How do you make your three-year-old feel loved and special when he keeps scrawling lipstick on your new wallpaper? How much thought can you give to your toddler's self-image when he has just dropped your wallet in the river?

As a child in a family of grown ups, you can't help but feel that everyone else knows everything and you don't. They all know about technical things like tying shoelaces and going to the toilet. You're the dummy who has to be told over and over. Big brothers and sisters don't help your self-image either. When they tell you you're stupid – and they're six and you're three – you have to believe them. They're experienced. They know about the world. They're SIX!

When you start school your problems multiply. Again it seems everyone else knows and you don't. Again, more comparisons. Teachers mostly ignore you when you do what's right and jump on you when you get it wrong. Again, you get a feeling that you're not OK. After eight or ten years of school, you hit puberty – and that's when things become really tough. Everything happens either too fast or too slow: things grow too big or not at all – and just being alive is enormously embarrassing.

Meanwhile, you're watching television daily. On TV, you see lots of talented and attractive people doing heroic things. The women have clean skin, big eyes and straight teeth, and the guys are six feet tall with square jaws and big biceps. When you compare yourself to these creatures, your self-image takes another thrashing.

Then there are the advertisements that tell us about all the things we have to have and can't afford. "Sophisticated people wear Christian Dior, women who "know" buy Gucci, men with style drive Jaguars ..." The message is, "If you haven't got this, then you haven't got IT." Meanwhile, your family continues to criticize you "because we love you." On Sundays you go to church to hear that you're a sinner.

Do you see what all this means? You hardly had a chance! By the time Mom, Dad, brother, sister, your math teacher, Uncle Ralph, Levi Strauss and the Brady Bunch have finished with you, you just don't measure up.

You don't match the "ideal". And there's a Catch 22. Most people around us have low self-esteem, so they pull us down, then we feel bad, and we pull them down, so they feel bad, and they pull us further down . . . We all end up feeling inferior. (One study indicated that even by fourteen years of age, 98 percent of children have a negative self-image. They hate their bodies; they feel inadequate and insecure.)

SO NOW THAT I KNOW WHERE I GOT MY POOR SELF-IMAGE, I CAN BLAME OTHER PEOPLE, RIGHT?

WRONG! Now that you know where some of your wild ideas came from, you can throw them out. DON'T BLAME PEOPLE. Your parents did the best job they knew how. They loved you the best way they knew how. Just understand that most of the messages you received about yourself were distorted. You got them from other people who felt they were never good enough, so what did they tell you? "YOU'RE NOT GOOD ENOUGH!" Your job is to begin to appreciate the real you.

"Wait a minute!", you say, "What if I'm really NOT very nice?" Well, if you don't think you're nice, you're probably still hanging onto that stuff that other people have told you.

"But," you say, "I object. I believe I SHOULD feel inadequate and guilty for the following reasons —

a) I've done a lot of stupid things.
b) I've disappointed people.
c) I often fail.
d) I feel that I'm not good enough.
e) I eat too much.
f) Sometimes I even have nasty thoughts."

Welcome to the human race! If you WERE perfect, you'd be an angel. The fact that you are still a person gives you permission to make some mistakes — and to be a little insecure like the rest of us.

DON'T SOME PEOPLE HAVE A GOOD SELF-IMAGE?

Yes, but they achieve high self-esteem by working at it, one day at a time. The irony is that even the people we most admire often feel inadequate. The football star takes his sporting talent for granted, and wishes that he was as brainy as his brother. His brainy brother gives himself little credit for making it through medical school, and wishes the women would find him as cute as his football playing sibling. They both wish they were as rich as cousin Charlie and Charlie wishes . . . This is the kind of topsy-turvy world we live in. The grass is always greener next door.

WHAT ABOUT PEOPLE WHO BOAST AND TELL YOU THEY'RE THE GREATEST?

No doubt you've met those people who believe they're the center of the whole universe – the ladies who genuinely believe they're some kind of Marilyn Monroe – Jackie Onassis – Eleanor Roosevelt rolled into one; the guys who give you the "I'm the greatest, richest, sexiest and smartest" routine within the first twenty three seconds of being introduced.

They are living proof that there is need for balance. Vanity irritates people. Those who brim with that artificial "I'm so wonderful" self-confidence, people who always have one eye in the mirror at parties, are turn-offs.

Notwithstanding those who really believe they're perfect, most people who continually tell us how wonderful they are, are really trying to convince themselves. They feel so fragile that to admit any weakness would be terrifying. They worry that if they ever stop advertising their accomplishments, the world might see the real "them".

As far as we're concerned, loving ourselves doesn't mean we should brag about ourselves. Rather, it is a matter of quiet self confidence, of self appreciation tempered with good humor, of inner stability.

Self-esteem is a delicate matter. Either too little or too much and you can be left feeling very alone.

HOW ELSE CAN I FEEL GOOD ABOUT ME?

In addition to a) avoiding continual self comparisons, b) setting mean-ingful, achievable goals and c) being more gentle with ourselves, there's something else we can do.

MAKE A NOTE OF THE CARING THINGS YOU DO. Quietly give yourself a pat on the back from time to time. There are a hundred things we may do in a day which contribute to the lives of those around us. Everytime you smile, listen, make someone a drink, collect your child from school, send a card, lend a friend a book, you're caring. Yet if someone

stopped you in the street and asked, "How did you help the planet today?", you might be stuck for words. It is so easy to forget, or to say, "I'm only doing what anyone else would do." Well, perhaps they are special people too – but don't discount your own contribution.

Too often we tell ourselves, "I'm doing no more than anyone should." Nonsense! Give yourself a pat on the back. Hold your head high and feel good. That's how you begin accomplishing more.

THERE'S HOPE FOR ALL OF US...

Ask anyone which qualities they most admire in people, and chances are you'll get a list including the following – honesty, determination, courage, commitment, persistence, a caring nature, generosity, and humility.

Take a close look at the list and you'll notice something. You aren't born with any of these qualities – you develop them. You aren't born courageous or honest or caring – you become that way if you really want to be that sort of person. You don't get these qualities by being LUCKY, you develop them if such assets are important enough to you.

Even knowledge and experience are not a matter of luck – and again, you aren't born with them. You go out and get them.

Isn't this exciting? What you are born with is of only moderate influence on your life's patterns. Far more significant are your personal goals. If you want to be bigger, stronger, more understanding or more determined, you can begin now – if you're serious. And as you grow and change, your self-image will change.

IN A NUTSHELL

The world is like a mirror. Most of the problems we have with people are a reflection of the problems we have with ourselves.

We don't have to go out and change everyone else. WHEN WE GENTLY CHANGE SOME OF OUR OWN IDEAS, OUR RELATIONSHIPS IMPROVE AUTOMATICALLY.

WAITING FOR SOMEONE...

" I'M JUST WAITING FOR SOMEONE TO COME ALONG AND MAKE ME HAPPY."

Mary is depressed and lonely. She feels her life is a mess. She tells herself, "If I can just find some people to like me I'll be happy." WRONG!

When your life is a mess, happy and stable people tend to avoid you. They look for those who are basically happy and stable. While Mary is miserable and depressed, she'll only attract people who have big problems. Then they'll have twice the misery.

The same applies to waiting for lovers. We have to sort ourselves out first. If I say to you, "Love me enough, and I'm sure I'll stop trying to kill myself," that's bound to put a strain on the relationship.

Other people can help to make us happier, but we need to be in control of our life first. When we wait for people to "arrive" and fix everything, we're courting disappointment —

• If they don't arrive, we get more depressed

• If they do arrive, but they don't behave as we want, then we get really depressed! Then we blame them and say, "you're supposed to make me happy!"

People who enjoy fulfilling, stable relationships are balanced people. They don't go looking for someone else to "fill a hole."

They recognize their own value. In songs and movies people say, "I was NOBODY 'till I met you," but in real life, that's an unhealthy situation. You have to be SOMEBODY first. It's no good being someone's "other half" — you're a whole person.

SO WHAT DO I DO?

Let's learn from Mary. She is lonely, depressed, and feels left out. She doesn't understand why people exclude her from their plans.

She may have overlooked the fact that she's always waiting for other people to call her up, make a move, make a date, and coax her into joining them. People get tired of coaxing you into things. They want enthusiasm.

You have to make it known that you're ready to participate in life. The first step in making friends is a willingness to get out and meet people. You don't meet many fascinating individuals walking between your TV and your refrigerator.

Mary can become an initiator, and get on the phone and call up some people..." Hi, Karen! You may not remember me but I live across the street. Would you like to go out for a pizza?" "Hi, Ted. I'm thinking of doing some cycling, studying, or hang gliding this weekend. Will you join me?"

The world is full of people who have conquered shyness (or arrogance) and have opened up new horizons. If you plan to make some changes and some new friends, be prepared for the occasional knockback or declined invitation. Continue to make the effort and you'll be well rewarded.

To avoid disappointment, form friendships without expecting anything in return. Do things for others without demands, and you'll never be disappointed. Some people will return favors and affection, and some won't. If you care for people because you want to, and not because you expect something back, you won't feel crushed should they fail to return a thought or a favor. The universe is essentially fair and just. If you are giving out care and affection, good things will come back to you, though not necessarily when or from where you expect.

IN A NUTSHELL

· We each must recognize our own value. If we depend on others to do it — and they don't — we're constantly disappointed.

· You can only complement someone else in a relationship if you're a complete person. Otherwise you're a drain on the relationship.

· If you're lonely and depressed, finding someone to like/love you won't help. Find someone to whom you can GIVE friendship without expectations.

· If you want to meet new people and make new friends, MAKE THE FIRST MOVE.

TAKING OURSELVES TOO SERIOUSLY

John had worn a beard for years and years, and decided he might shave it off. But he was self-conscious about making the change and wondered, "What will all my friends and workmates say? Will they joke about my face?"

After months of deliberation, he finally gathered the courage to remove the fluff — at least, he removed all but the hair on his upper lip. Fearing the worst, he arrived at work next day. To his surprise, nobody said anything about his "new look". In fact, by lunchtime nobody had said a word.

Finally, he could stand it no longer. He raised the subject himself — "What do you think of my new look?"

They looked blank, "What look?"

"Don't you notice anything different about me?"

There was a long silence while they all studied him from head to toe. Finally, someone chirped up, "Yeah, you've grown a moustache!"

Isn't it true that we can take ourselves so seriously, being very self-conscious and thinking everyone is looking at us, yet nobody else is even giving us a thought?

Taking ourselves too seriously can also mean desperately trying to make an impression. Take Nina, who spends two hours dolling herself up every time she leaves the house. She agonizes over the blue suit and the satin dress, over the black pumps and the white sandals. She tries eleven different necklaces and seventeen pairs of earrings before she gets the right effect. She turns to her husband, "How do I look?"

"Great."

"Are you sure?"

"Fantastic."

"Hair not too severe?"

"No, it's perfect."

"Lipstick not too dark?"

"Beautiful."

"You're sure I look OK?"

"You look lovely."

Between the front door and the car, Nina rushes back to the bedroom. To change her earrings. Two or three times in the course of the evening, she tells herself (sometimes she whispers it to her husband) — " I should have used the pearl studs instead." Her husband says, " It doesn't matter." And Nina gets hurt.

There's a point at which pride in appearance becomes an obsession. Hers is an example of low self-esteem working in reverse – she's not nearly so interested in making friends as making an impression. Nina's world revolves around her shoes, her clothes, her taste in jewelry and herself. When other people seem remote, she figures they're intimidated or envious. Actually, they find her painful and boring.

So often, things that are hugely important to us don't matter at all to the rest of humanity. Brian gets a pimple on the end of his nose, and sentences himself to a week of solitary confinement. Who cares?

IN A NUTSHELL

Bring to mind the people with whom you love to spend time. Chances are they're people who can laugh at themselves. People who laugh at themselves have more fun, more friends and less ulcers.

When we're too self-conscious, others feel embarrassed, and ultimately, we cut them off.

SORTING YOURSELF OUT

A sweet life is a shared experience.

THE DISTANCE WE KEEP

"WE ARE ALL SO MUCH TOGETHER BUT WE ARE ALL DYING OF LONELINESS."
– Dr. Albert Schweitzer

Consider our twentieth century lifestyle - how we secure ourselves against unwelcome personal invasion. Many of us live in high rise apartments where we meet the neighbors once a month in the lobby. Others reside in the suburbs, surrounded by high fences and security systems. We have private telephone numbers and guard dogs at the gate. We consciously eliminate the possibility of any unhappy encounters – but we have managed to cut out lots of the happy ones too.

We spend three hours a day in traffic jams – isolated. We talk to computers. We don't go to see people; we send faxes.

Shopping malls have replaced the corner store. TV dinners have replaced the family dinner – or we simply eat at the refrigerator.

When we go to public places, we take our blank stares. Blank stares are standard equipment for distancing yourself in elevators, subway trains, and supermarkets. The blank look says, "I don't know you, there's nothing happening in my head, don't talk to me 'cause you might be a weirdo."

We watch four hours of television a day – alone. No matter if there are others in the room, our concern is with the TV. We have video recorders to help us out – if there is nothing on the airwaves, we can still get an electronic fix.

Is all this bad? No. It is not necessarily bad. We live in exciting (and very convenient) times, but we need to understand what is happening. There are enormous pressures pulling us away from people. If you want personal contact these days, you have to make an effort.

A sweet life is a shared experience. Our greatest joys, our most precious moments, our toughest challenges and our most loving times are mostly shared with people. Our greatest learning experiences come from being with people.

To have a memorable stay on this planet we must be prepared to knock down some barriers – make a special effort to meet, be with, get close to people.

A father may be heard to say, "I don't spend much time with the kids, but what I spend is QUALITY time."

Quality time has to be quantity time. If ten-year-old Johnny wants to read you his book, or take you for a walk or roll with you on the grass, you can't say, "Let's have a quality two-minute-walk" or a "a quality fifty-eight second-roll." It's only a quality thing if you both do it 'till you're finished. Let's not kid ourselves.

We have to work at spending time with people, and make it a priority. The tide of technology always tugs us in the opposite direction.

QUIT PLAYING GAMES

No-one can make it all alone, though sometimes we fake it. We pretend we can. But there are no prizes for spending a lifetime playing games, saying, "I'm OK. I don't need anyone."

What a shame it is when pride gets in the way. Jane says, "I would call up Bob but I wouldn't want him to think I like him!" Bob says, "I'm mad about Jane but I could never tell her!" They spend weekends by themselves, proud but lonely.

There is no shame in finding someone else to be attractive, or good company. Even if they don't like you, there is still no shame. If you happen to be fond of someone, and they're not fond of you, it's OK. You don't have to have them like you first, or tell you first. You don't have to wait to see if they'll love you back! You can announce it – say, "Hey! I think you're a fantastic person. Regardless of what you think about me, that's how I feel about you."

Joy in life comes from expressing ourselves, in taking risks and jumping in. Everyone is not going to like you but you can like who you like.

Jim looks forward to seeing his girl all week. Thursday night he polishes his car, puts on his best shirt and after-shave, drives twenty five miles across town, knocks on her door and says, "Hi! I happened to be in the neighborhood . . ."

Dammit Jim, tell her the real story. Say, "I've been waiting a week for this. The time wouldn't go quick enough. I couldn't wait to see you. I was so excited, I sang love songs all along the freeway." Tell her that you almost called her on twenty different occasions, but you were worried she'd think you foolish.

This sort of honesty takes a little courage and it's a part of being fully human. It lets us see inside ourselves. It sparks new relationships and revives old ones.

You say, "But shouldn't I play hard to get?" Well, that's one way to operate, but there are better ways of developing bonds with people – like being yourself, or being refreshingly open.

The song says, "People who need people are the luckiest people in the world." It might also have said "people who need people and pretend they don't are the biggest losers."

"BUT I DON'T WANT TO BE HURT..."

Isn't that a great excuse? "I don't want to be hurt. I don't want to get too close because eventually they'll leave me or die, and then I'll be shattered." Sure you'll be shattered, but how much better to be shattered with the thought, "We gave it everything we had!"

The ones who really suffer are those who know inside that things could have been much better, closer, more exciting – but they weren't.

ATTRACTING PEOPLE

A fellow lamented to his buddy – "I'm always having disasters and people keep letting me down! Why is that?"

His friend thought for a moment and replied, "Well, as I figure it, you're just the kind of person that rotten things happen to!"

Don't we all know people who are always getting let down by their friends? Don't we know others who are constantly surrounded by supportive friends – and people who always seem to get treated with respect?

Why do some of us get treated well and others badly? There seem to be two major possibilities. Either –

a) It is all a matter of luck, or

b) We cause what happens to us – and if we keep behaving the same way, we keep getting the same results.

I notice that some people succeed (and others fail), with such monotonous regularity that there has to be something more than luck at work. Let's investigate possibility "b".

HOW CAN I BE CAUSING WHAT'S HAPPENING TO ME?

From the moment we are born, we begin to make up our mind about the world. Having had no previous experience of life, we draw our first major conclusions about "what life is like" from our birth experience and our subsequent few years as a little person.

Psychologists agree that by the time we are five, much of our personality has been formed. By then we've developed some fixed beliefs about ourselves and the rest of the world - eg. "I'm nice", "I'm rotten", "I cause trouble", "people love me when I'm clever", "I'm cute", "You can't trust men", "I'm funny", "People rip you off" . . .

Some of these beliefs we hold consciously, and others are buried deep in our subconscious. Having formed these beliefs, they rule us, and WE SPEND OUR WHOLE LIVES PROVING THAT WHAT WE BELIEVE IS CORRECT. Sometimes we manage to wreck our lives, but at least we prove we're right!

Let's look at some examples of how we may live our lives to fit our belief system.

MARY

Mary doesn't feel good about herself. She expects others to agree with her poor self-image and kick her around. Along comes Fred who treats her well. This makes her feel uncomfortable.

She thinks, "He is a little too friendly – he must be a bit strange to be so nice to ME. She reasons, "If he likes me, I bet there's something wrong with him. I'd better brush him off!" Fred gets the message that he is not welcome, and leaves. Mary laments, "Where are all the nice people in my life?"

MATTHEWS.

Enter Ted the Terror. Ted is a bully. Ted fits Mary's belief system which says "men kick you around". He kicks her around, so she figures he is a regular guy. She is comfortable with Ted the Terror. She lives unhappily ever after, and is able to say to all her friends, "Men are rotten and I can prove it. Look at Ted!"

LOUISE

Louise grows up in a gentle, loving environment. Her family and her family's friends are caring people. She has a positive self-image.

She chooses caring friends. In fact, when she meets rude and aggressive people, she feels uncomfortable, and looks for other company. When she meets a man who behaves like a gorilla, she says to herself, "This guy has a problem. I know there are people out there who will treat me better than this. I will spend my time with them." Louise spends her life proving her belief system which says, "I can always find caring people to be with." Louise leaves the gorillas for Mary.

MARTIN

Martin grows up an independent little fellow. His parents give him little support and he learns to do everything on his own. Everyone thinks, "Martin is so independent – he doesn't need any help." Martin looks around and thinks, "Nobody gives me any support – if I want anything done, I have to do it myself."

Martin starts a business. He employs people who are unsupportive because he believes "useless people are normal." When he accidentally employs someone who is helpful and motivated, there is always a personality clash. He feels they're pushy and they feel he's always "taking over". The good staff leave and the useless ones stay. Martin the Martyr continues to do everyone else's work.

Enter incapable Millie. She falls in love with good old hard working, capable Martin. They fit perfectly – she admires him; he does everything for her, and resents her for it. Ask Martin about the human race and he'll tell you straight, "People are useless. I ought to know – I'm surrounded by useless people."

JOHN

Let's look at John, who is constantly getting into trouble.

John was a neighbor of mine, and some years back, we went to a bar together. We had been at the bar about twenty minutes, when I noticed there was a fight going on in the corner. A fellow was having the life choked out of him, and it was John.

I went over and politely asked the fellow who was strangling John to let him go. Eventually he agreed, and John and I left for another bar. We arrived at the second nightspot, and I went to the men's room. Returning to the bar, I saw a crowd of people around a pool table thumping somebody. It was John again!

As I dragged him out to the car, he proceeded to tell me about another great night spot we should visit. He explained to me about the fights. He said, "People are out to get you, so you have to hit them first."

John expects others to be aggressive. With his tunnel vision he focuses on pugnacious people. He works in a job where people want to beat him up, and he goes to nightspots where he gets thumped – again in accordance with his beliefs. It's very painful, but John is out there proving his belief system too.

You say, "Wouldn't Mary rather prove her beliefs wrong so she can live happily ever after?" "Wouldn't John consider changing his beliefs, so that other people will stop breaking his nose?" "Wouldn't Martin rather change to believing that people will help him out?" They might change, but our beliefs are precious things. For centuries, men have been suffering and dying in their millions for what they believe. Lots of us are still doing it.

We each say, "I KNOW I'M RIGHT!", but we can be so close to our own situation that we don't see what is happening. Being RIGHT becomes more important to us than being happy.

We each need to ask ourselves, "What do I believe about life, relationships and people, and how has this been determining what I get?"

WHAT ABOUT SITUATIONS IN WHICH YOU HAVE NO CONTROL?

We have a lot more control over our life than we may admit. On a conscious level, we include or exclude people from our life, but we ALSO do it subconsciously. Our mind is like a magnet, and depending on our thoughts, we attract certain people into our world.

Think about it. Have you ever spent the morning thinking about an old friend and bumped into him in the street that very afternoon? Have you ever particularly NOT wanted to meet someone – an old girlfriend, your mother – and then met her in the most unlikely and embarrassing circumstances? Have you ever stumbled across a teacher or an employer or a future wife and later thought to yourself – "It was so unlikely to have found him (her) but so right. It must have been meant to happen?" Have you ever, as you emerged from a period of depression, suddenly found some wonderful, uplifting friends and said to yourself, "Now that I'm ready for people like this, here they are?"

With our thoughts, we pull people to us. If you believe that everyone wants to abuse you, you'll find people to do it – or they'll find you ... on the street, in parking lots, on the telephone, in aircraft ... If you believe that people are kind and friendly, somehow they'll more offen than not appear this way.

In Mary's case, she not only prefers to be stuck with the Teds of the world, she has an internal radar to find them. If there's one Ted at a party, she'll sniff him out. Similarly, Louise will find her kind of people, Martin will find his, and John will intuitively know where to go to get punched in the face.

WHAT IS THE POINT OF ALL THIS? IT DOESN'T SEEM FAIR!

Life is a learning experience and one of the classes we take is relationships. The universe serves us the lessons to learn; if we don't learn, we get to take the class over. Sometimes we take the class again with the same person, or sometimes with a new person with the same old problem.

For example, Martin's lesson may be to learn to depend on other people. If he learns to do this, perhaps through learning to respect and manage others, he'll eventually stop working himself into the ground. If he never changes his attitude and beliefs, he'll spend the rest of his life creating situations where he does all the work. (And proving that he's right!)

Likewise, Mary and John may choose to remain locked-in to their particular patterns, or they may choose to change their attitudes and their life's experiences as a result.

IN A NUTSHELL

While a belief system is holding you back, you keep creating opportunities for yourself to learn about it. Once you make a breakthrough, you don't have to keep learning the same lesson, and your life changes.

STOP PASSING THE BUCK

People who make friends easily don't spend their time blaming other people.

If I take you out for a meal, and spend the evening blaming my family, my boss, the neighborhood – and you – for my depressed lifestyle, you won't be holding your breath for my next dinner invitation, will you?"

If you choose to spend time with me, you'll be hoping that my company will make your life richer and more enjoyable – that you'll FEEL GOOD when you're with me.

So here's a major reason for avoiding constantly finding fault with the world – your friends soon tire of you. The other reason for taking responsibility for our own lives is equally sound – while we keep blaming other people, our life will never work.

When you're three years old, blaming people is a useful strategy. If you can blame your brother for breaking the bedroom window, it becomes his problem, and you avoid a spanking.

The problem is that later in life, punishment is not the question. Learning is the question. Every time you blame someone else, you don't learn and things don't change.

Listen to couples on the brink of divorce, interview an unsuccessful businessman, speak to a failing student, and you'll hear phrases like –

"It's not my fault."

"I can't help it."

"It's my teacher's fault."

"You should have told me. It's your fault."

"No one else understands me."

"It's the government's fault. They should do something."

"They let me down."

"Nobody cares about me."

"It's my mother's fault."

It's losers' talk, and the common thread is, "this situation is not my fault so I'm not going to correct it." Unfortunately, while we blame others, the problem never gets solved, so blamers remain frustrated and miserable.

HAPPY PEOPLE TAKE FULL RESPONSIBILITY

If you want happy friendships, you have to take responsibility. Even if you figure it is your parents' fault that you got a bad start to life, decide that it is up to you to do something now. If you had a string of rotten teachers, and you can't count or spell, take responsibility. If you work with a bunch of people who are driving you crazy, it is up to you to stay happy. If YOU don't fix your life, who will?

It is easy to fall into the trap of blaming others. Pop songs do it all the time - ". . . you broke my heart . . ," ". . . you made me cry . . ," ". . . you left me lonely. . ," ". . . you wrecked my life and if you don't come back I'll shoot myself . . ."

NOBODY CAN MAKE YOU MISERABLE WITHOUT YOUR PERMISSION. No matter what someone says or does, you decide how you will react. If your boss fires you or your brother-in-law says you are too fat, they haven't made you unhappy. They have simply given you choices of how to respond.

Not blaming also means taking responsibility for our actions. How often do we pretend to be the innocent party? We use phrases like, "I got this feeling," "I fell into a depression," "I couldn't do anything about it." The truth is usually not that we COULD'NT but that we DIDN'T.

If we're honest with ourselves, we're always choosing — where we are, whom we're with, what we're saying, how we're reacting. We're choosing about everything in our life — our company, our job, our spouse, what we think.

As soon as we admit that we're CHOOSING — and that it's up to us — the sooner we begin to live fully.

I know a university professor who regards himself as highly intelligent. He works 70 hours per week and hates every minute of it. He said to me,

"I hate my job and I'm caught in the rat race — but what can I do?"

What can he do? DO SOMETHING ABOUT IT! DO SOMETHING ELSE! He has one life to live. He is fifty years old, he is a leading academic, but he hasn't figured out how to spend his time doing something he enjoys. How intelligent is that? He pretends he has no choice in the matter and so refuses to change his attitude or his job.

YOU DECIDE HOW YOU FEEL

One aspect of dealing with people effectively is not letting them get you down. Misery can be contagious. Sometimes people will even insist that you should be depressed.

Recently my house was robbed. The thieves took a video recorder, two hundred dollars in cash, a bucketful of loose change and an old suitcase.

I decided, after the initial upsetting realization that we had been ripped off, that no petty thief was going to wreck my day. The experience was irritating, but also enlightening. On reflection, I was even relieved to be rid of the suitcase.

Guess what the biggest problem was! Other people wanted me to be depressed. My friend Jim found out and became quite insistent that I should be disturbed.

Jim felt he was commiserating, and I hesitated to shut out someone who believed he was being supportive. I said, "Jim, you heard we were burgled and I guess you know all the facts. You also know that I like to put unpleasantness behind me as soon as I can, so thank you for your concern and let me tell you about something much more interesting . . ." (Jim did me the favor of telling his friends, and soon I had more people approaching me with long faces . . . "I heard your house was robbed. You must feel terrible").

Often others mean well, but manage to help you feel worse. It is up to us to decide how we feel. Have you ever been working or playing or teaching and had someone come to you and say, "Gee, you must be tired!" Being tired was the last thing on your mind, until you were reminded.

Similarly, we need to guard against instructions to be disappointed. Your brother forgets your birthday and someone says, "You must be hurt!" YOU decide how you feel. Maybe you'll decide that he could forget all your birthdays and it wouldn't make a bit of difference.

TELL PEOPLE WHAT YOU WANT

Another aspect of blaming/taking responsibility is telling people what you want.

Brad takes Wendy dancing. Just before midnight, Wendy turns to Brad and says, "I didn't want to come dancing. I wanted to see a movie."

Brad, "But you said, let's go dancing!"

Wendy, "That's because I thought you'd want to go dancing. I wanted to see a movie."

Brad, "You never even mentioned movies."

Wendy, "That's got nothing to do with it."

Brad, "Why didn't you tell me you wanted to see a movie?"

Wendy, "You should have asked."

It's up to us to communicate clearly – "This is what I want," – and not to blame others if we're having a bad time.

In healthy relationships, the partners express their wants and needs – "I want this," "I like to be touched that way," "Please help me here," "I want you to listen carefully to this . . ."

Also, the people we like the most are the people who don't blame us for things. So that's another reason why blaming is a bad idea – our friends hate it!

"THE WORLD OWES ME A LIVING SYNDROME"

One consequence of bulk blaming is "the world owes me a living syndrome." This manifests in statements like "why don't people appreciate me?", "why hasn't anyone discovered my talents?" and "life shouldn't be this difficult – somebody should do something."

The healthiest approach is to figure that the world doesn't owe us anything. Life is like a big supermarket where you are one of five billion products in the store. Your challenge is to represent value to other people – value in terms of being good company and in terms of being useful to people. If you represent good value, you will be in demand with friends and employers. If you're a liability, you get left on the shelf.

As an artist I have met numerous struggling artists who blame everybody but themselves for their difficulties. They say, "What is the matter with the public? Don't they appreciate art?" or "I'm an artist! I'm creative. Society should support me!"

Rubbish! Why should society support you if they hate your paintings?

Living on this planet is a privilege. If we want to enjoy the nice things of life, it is up to us to represent value to other people.

BLAMING USUALLY BECOMES AN EXCUSE NOT TO ACT, AND INACTION NEVER HELPED ANYBODY.

It doesn't matter how long your blame list is – whether it includes your children, your education, parents, rotten neighbors, the government, the weather – if you are miserable, it is no consolation. REASONS OR EXCUSES ARE NEVER ANY CONSOLATION. AT THE END OF THE DAY ALL THAT COUNTS IS WHETHER YOU GOT WHERE YOU REALLY WANTED TO GO.

IN A NUTSHELL

Happy and successful people succeed in spite of difficulties. Not in the absence of difficulties. While "blamers" concentrate on the problem, you concentrate on the solution. Ask yourself, a) "What do I want?" and b) "What action will I take to get it?"

People will tell you from time to time, "You should be upset," "Times are tough," "Life is a bummer", "Work is a pain in the neck." Tell yourself quietly, "That is their reality, and I respect it, and I may choose to talk with them about it – but I refuse to adopt it. I CHOOSE HOW I FEEL."

HONESTY PAYS OFF

Mary has a problem. She says to her friend, "Harry wants to take me out. He is a nice enough guy but we have nothing in common. I don't want to go. What do I tell him?" Mary and her friend agonize over what to say.

It is really not that complicated, Mary. What you say is, "Harry, you are a nice enough guy but we have nothing in common. I don't want to go." Isn't it simple? Why complicate life?

Another alternative . . . "Harry, I've been agonizing over what to say to you. I even asked my friend about how to tell you this – you see, I think you're a nice guy but I don't want to date you."

Honesty makes things so simple. It's not that humanity will love you more if you don't tell lies, but that honesty, with tact, is the easiest solution.

Let's say that your boss has asked you to post some important letters. Instead of mailing them, you accidently threw them out with the trash. You could go to great lengths to create stories and excuses, but it makes life so difficult. Isn't it easier to say, "Boss, I've been a complete idiot. It is no fun telling you this but your proposals are now at the local dump!"

When you are honest with people –
- they admire and appreciate you
- they trust you
- they know where you stand
- you can get more of what you want

Don't you appreciate people giving it to you straight?

A fellow came to see me recently. He hung around for a couple of hours, asking questions like, "what are you doing?", "are you busy?" and "how is business?" I figured he was on a social visit. Days later I learned that he had just lost his job and he wanted work. Had he said, "I lost my job and I want some work.", I could have helped him. Isn't it strange? The man wouldn't even tell me that he wanted work. Meanwhile, he couldn't pay his rent.

If you want something, say it. "I want help," "I want to borrow a hundred dollars," "I want you to stop hassling me." If you want to date somebody, tell her. You say, "You are the most fascinating person at this whole party. I would like to take you out. What do you say?"

Kids get what they want because they ask for it. It is part of their charm. When we are honest like children, people find us more charming too.

Also, if you don't know something, be honest about it. It is so exasperating listening to teachers, colleagues, parents, and other "experts" who pretend to have all the answers. People always respect the person who is able to say, "I don't know."

IN A NUTSHELL

Be tactful and tell it like it is. Honesty with others is a sign of respect for them and a sign of self respect – and it's so much simpler!

EXPRESSING ANGER

I t is natural to feel angry from time to time. Unfortunately, most of us are taught that it is not nice to get angry – parents and teachers don't know how to handle it and they're embarrassed and awkward when someone is yelling and screaming.

Therefore, most of us are taught "never get angry, don't show your displeasure." By adulthood, many of us have learned not to be angry with people anymore – we have learned how to punish ourselves instead.

EXAMPLE – You and I spend an evening together. You talk the whole time, and I can't get a word in. I'm angry and frustrated that you won't shut your mouth even for a minute.

Do I tell you, "I'm angry because..." No! That wouldn't be nice. So I get drunk instead – and then stew over your behavior for the next week.

EXAMPLE – You promise to collect me from work at 5:00pm. You arrive at 7:30. I'm extremely upset that you have no respect for my time. But do I tell you "I'm angry because...?" Probably not. That wouldn't be nice. So I spend the evening criticizing you and your clothes and your job and your friends and I manage to wreck the evening for both of us.

EXAMPLE – You don't seem to be interested in anything I do. Whenever I try to talk about my hobbies or my plans, you change the subject. I know that nice people don't get angry, so I get depressed instead – perhaps for a week, maybe for a year or two.

With my depression come headaches, stomach pains, listlessness and so on. Now I'm sick, but at least I didn't get angry!

EXAMPLE – I'm upset about lots of things and people in my life.

But I don't want to get angry with them because then they wouldn't like me. So I eat. I can't express myself so I punish myself.

I've simplified these examples, but they represent familiar patterns. It may be difficult to express anger, and it can upset other people temporarily, but when we express our anger there is a chance to fix the problem. Suppressing our displeasure only creates more problems.

SO HOW DO I EXPRESS ANGER?

Understand that often others won't like it but you're acting in everyone's best interest. Also —

- Take responsibility for how you feel. Say "I feel angry about . . ." rather than "You're a jerk . . ."
- If necessary, wait a few minutes (or hours), to cool off so you can speak with a clear head.
- Be very positive with the other person where possible. For example,. "I really appreciate you picking me up from work and I know you had to go out of your way...when you arrive two hours late, I feel angry...I'm not criticizing you, I just want you to know how I feel."

Before finishing the subject of anger . . . its suppression or expression . . . there are two aspects — one of which I briefly touched on above — that I want you to consider in greater depth before we move to the next topic.

43

The first is the preference for clear-headed anger and by this I am suggesting an important measure of control. In other words, you are angry ... perhaps, very angry ... but:

YOU RETAIN FULL CONTROL OF YOUR EMOTIONS.

It is an intelligent move to break away from the immediate environment of concern for a cooling-off period. A long walk around the block or in a nearby park may suffice. But wherever you choose to go, bear in mind the commitment to yourself. You are not opting out. Rather you are withdrawing to gain perspective.

Equally important at this time is your recognition of the fact that you are not some battered military unit, seeking rest and recuperation before re-launching yourself headlong into the fray. You are, instead, looking to resolve the conflict, not to establish victory.

IT IS REASONABLE TO EXPRESS ANGER. BUT ONLY IF YOU REMAIN RATIONAL.

The other point I would like you to consider, when expressing anger, is the importance of sticking to the immediate source of current aggravation. By this means you are seeking to contain the seriousness of the concern.

Again, remember, you want resolution, not victory. Don't drag in past events that have been settled or shelved long ago.

Take care to avoid involving other people or circumstances, no matter how relevant they may appear to be at the moment. Such tactics are invariably cheap means of scoring points. They inevitably complicate issues, make solutions that much more difficult, and further dent relationships.

IN A NUTSHELL

When you get angry, people may not like it but they get over it soon enough, and you'll understand each other better. When you don't get angry – and you punish yourself instead – the problem remains and the damage is much worse.

CHAPTER 3

SIMPLIFY YOUR LIFE

Our Expectations

Assert Yourself

Leave People To Their Own Thoughts

Stop Explaining Your Life

When You Want To Say " NO!"

"What other people think of you is none of your business."

OUR EXPECTATIONS

YOU ARE RESPONSIBLE FOR HOW THE WORLD TREATS YOU.

If you don't like what you are getting, change what you are doing – it's up to you to teach people how you want to be treated. Too often we blame the other guy. If a partnership isn't working, if a relationship is failing, you're responsible too. If someone is walking all over you, it's half your fault.

Let's take Helen, who gets pushed around by her husband. She laments, "I am a doormat to my husband, Brutus. I just follow orders. He never helps me at home, we only go where he wants to go, Brutus never gives me any money for myself. He treats me like dirt, never appreciates anything I do." Helen has one of those "what have I done to deserve this?" martyr complexes.

So you ask Helen, "Why don't you stand up to the Brute?" Helen says, "I did once and he lost his temper and put his fist through the bathroom door. I realized then that it wasn't worth the trouble. I just go along with what he wants."

Helen may not realize it, or admit it, but she has trained Brutus. You can bet he doesn't bully everybody; just those who allow it. Until now, Helen has taken the easiest option – taking no responsibility, being weak, basking in the sympathy of her friends while lumping all the blame on Brutus the Barbarian. Should Helen change the way she reacts to her husband, Brutus might soon become house trained!

What should Helen do? Firstly, she can begin to respect herself. OTHERS RESPECT US TO THE DEGREE THAT WE RESPECT OURSELVES. When Brutus senses that Helen expects to be treated well, he will begin to change his tune. People who get pushed around radiate an attitude which says, "I bet you are going to kick me around — and I'll let you do it — and then I'll blame you for it."

Helen has lots of options. She can say, "Brutus, if you ever put your fist through the bathroom door again, I'll move out for a month," and be prepared to do it. She may calmly let him know that from now on she chooses to be treated like a human being. She may decide that she no longer wants to live with a gorilla and leave for good.

In any relationship, it takes two to tango. Both parties are responsible, and both parties receive certain payoffs for their particular role. Helen's payoffs are that she gets to avoid responsibility, avoids making tough decisions and gets to blame Brutus for everything. Brutus, on the other hand has a slave, gets what he wants and gets to blame his wife for everything.

It takes two to make a relationship work and it takes two to make it break down. Somehow, though, it is a lot easier to be objective about

another couple's problems than it is our own! One particular couple I know live on the brink of divorce. She stays home out of choice. She reads novels and sleeps. She doesn't cook and never cleans the house. He believes that there should be food on the table when he gets home from the factory. There never is any food ready, so he shouts, screams and tears the house apart. He believes he's living with a lazy, good for nothing slob – and that she is a hundred percent in the wrong. She figures she's stuck with a mental case and that it is all his fault. I suppose the lesson that we learn here is that whenever we think that it is all our partner's fault, IT ISN'T.

On any street you'll find families where the kids run the house. They order the parents about ... "Dad! Get my socks" ... "Mom, bring me some cake" ... "Iron my shirt" ... "Take me to baseball NOW"...

The parents ask themselves, "What did we do to deserve this?" Answer. They ran around after their kids for fifteen years. They taught the children how to treat them – like slaves!

You have to train your children. If an eight-year-old can operate a computer, he can run a dishwasher. If he's clever enough to ride a skate board, he can iron a shirt.

Teach the kids that you're not their servants and give them a sense of contribution.

Have you ever heard a mother say, "No one in my family ever says THANK YOU"? How does that happen? It happens when mother doesn't stand up for herself and doesn't teach the kids how to treat her. She laments, "My six children are grown up and married. Not once did they ever say THANK YOU for anything."

What if, years ago, she had said to her little ones, "In our family, THANK YOU is a sign of appreciation and respect. When I cook you dinner, I expect you to say thank you. If you forget to thank me for Thursday's dinner, you'll cook Friday's dinner. If you don't thank me for a ride to baseball, you walk the next week". Assuming she was true to her word, wouldn't the children learn manners in a hurry?

DEALING WITH PEOPLE WHO IMPOSE

Have you ever had people arrive at your door who didn't know when to leave? Maybe they stayed until four in the morning – or maybe they stayed 'till Christmas. We need to be able to deal with such people without stress – to be comfortable about saying, "This isn't convenient..."

Similarly, others may make a habit of monopolizing our time. If you want to give them the time, fine. But avoid those situations where you give people your time, smile a lot, and then resent them for the next week. We shouldn't mistake self sacrifice for politeness.

Some people will happily bore you to death with endless stories which you've heard a dozen times over. Unless you take action to re-route the conversation, or at least ask for an abridged version of their dramas, they will show you no mercy. Sure, be courteous and friendly, but if neighbor Frank starts on his three-hour 1962 prostate operation saga, you may want to cut him off.

Have respect for your own time, and while being polite, feel comfortable about stating your case..." Frank, I appreciate you taking the time to tell me this story. It may surprise you to know that you've told me this story before," or "I don't have much time right now. Can you just give me the essentials of the story?"

Similarly with crybabies and whiners, you don't have to submit yourself to endless complaining. Take a stand. You may like to say, "I don't believe your current approach is helping either of us. Let's look at doing something constructive to stem the problem."

Some people take delight in making you feel guilty..."If it weren't for you...You are letting me down... After all I have done for you..." Don't wear it. Guilt is destructive. Draw their attention to what they are doing and ask them outright, "You aren't trying to make me feel guilty, are you?" Usually they'll get the message and quit.

IN A NUTSHELL

If others give you no respect, monopolize your time, or walk all over you, ask yourself, "What am I doing to encourage people to treat me like this?" If you want them to change, YOU have to change.

ASSERT YOURSELF

IF YOU LET YOURSELF BE PUSHED AROUND BY THOSE YOU LOVE, YOU'LL END UP RESENTING THEM FOR IT.

Where do you draw the line between assertive and aggressive behavior? When are we taking a fair stand, and when are we being offensive?

The line may be a fine one, but one thing is for sure – you have a duty to yourself and to your loved ones to assert yourself. When we internalize our problems, and play "victim", we're heading for big trouble.

Asserting yourself isn't a matter of morality. It is usually not even a question of "rights." It is simply a matter of you, as a fully functioning person, being able to make a stand for what you want.

People often talk in terms of "their rights". John says, "I have a right to fair treatment, a right to good service, a right to receive respect!" But it is not an issue of rights. It is a matter of what you choose to do about getting the treatment that you want.

Laws of nature don't seem particularly concerned about specific rights. They don't ordain how much a plumber should charge to change a washer in your bathroom. Nor do they deliberate at a level that would influence the actions of a bank teller who is being rude to you. Nor, for that matter, would they sway your boss' decision one way or another on your salary increase.

Your task as an effective person is simply to decide what is right for you – and then take your stand. If you want to reprimand a waiter for dropping his glasses in your soup, OK. If you don't want to make any more waves, that's OK too.

There are no laws written in the sky which say, "Thou shalt not complain about rude taxi drivers" or "Thou shalt complain about thy husband's choice of TV program" or "Thou shalt happily accept abuse from waiters." ELIMINATE ANY SENSE OF BEING EITHER A "BAD PERSON" OR A "GOOD PERSON" SHOULD YOU CHOOSE TO BE ASSERTIVE.

In being assertive, the following guidelines will help you achieve results –

a) BE OBJECTIVE. When you complain about a situation, don't exaggerate or hurl blame. eg. When someone is smoking next to you in a restaurant, you might say, "Your smoke is blowing in my face while I'm

eating. Would you please be so kind as not to smoke?" Such an approach is preferable to the "take your dirty habit outside!" technique.

Too often we say "you ALWAYS" or "you NEVER." eg. "You're always late!" "You never listen!" Such generalizations offend people. Similarly, it is important that we are fair and accurate with our assessment — "your filthy smoke is choking me to death" might be an offensive exaggeration.

b) TAKE RESPONSIBILITY FOR HOW YOU FEEL. "You make such a noise with your spaghetti, I find it difficult to enjoy my meal. I feel upset that people in the restaurant are staring at you." instead of "You are making me sick. You should be arrested!"

It is important to recognize that we choose our reactions and not blame others. Use words like "I feel irritated" or "it concerns me" instead of "you make me sick" or "you're a pig."

c) BE CLEAR ABOUT WHAT YOU WANT. eg. "I would like to see the manager of this store immediately," or "Before I pay the bill, I would like an itemized statement of labor and material costs."

Tell people specifically. Vague instructions like "Smarten up!" or "Learn some manners!" or "Stop ripping me off!" don't help.

d) STATE CONSEQUENCES. eg. In confronting a neighbor over his blaring music, "If you'll turn down your stereo a little, I'll make sure I do the same next time we have a party."

State the benefits you'll both enjoy if they decide to take action. Talk in terms of "positives if you do" rather than "negatives if you don't." It is also helpful to offer to make an effort on your part in return for their efforts.

When we do choose to be assertive, it is in our own best interest that we treat people with respect, for we reap in life what we sow. We get back what we put out. If your neighbor's blaring stereo system is keeping you awake every night, you'll probably want to assert yourself. Whether or not he turns down the volume has a lot more to do with your communication skills than it does with your "rights" and what is "fair".

IN ADDITION . . . When asserting yourself, be firm. Don't start by apologizing eg. "I'm sorry to bother you but your car is parked on my foot." Apologizing tells people you are a wimp. There is no need to be sorry — just tell them what they need to know.

Also, you'll have the best chance of getting results if you only complain about one thing at a time. This is basic information but sometimes we get carried away, for example, "Stop eating like a pig, quit moaning, pull yourself together, sober up, get a proper job and start helping around the house" could be a bit much to handle. Fix the eating first and negotiate from there.

BRUSH OFFS

Sometimes you'll assert yourself and people will try and brush you off with familiar phrases –

"No one else has complained!"

"Aren't you being a bit petty?"

"I don't have time to talk right now."

You need to know how to respond, perhaps with phrases like –

"Well I'm complaining now because I consider it important."

"I do not consider it petty..."

"Give me a specific time when you will talk."

IN A NUTSHELL

When you assert yourself, be objective. Take responsibility for how you feel and be specific about what you want. You'll win some and you'll lose some. When you win, you demonstrate that you can take control of situations and get what you want. When you lose, usually you'll feel better for having expressed your feelings.

But Be Flexible...

Having learned how to say "no", remember that there will be times when it pays to accommodate other people — to fit in with their plans..

Some interruptions to our crowded schedules could actually be needed breaks. Be prepared for them. Think before saying, "no, thank you." As always, our challenge is to strike an harmonious balance.

LEAVE PEOPLE TO THEIR OWN THOUGHTS

"What other people think of you is none of your business."

I used to donate to absolutely anything. If I was walking down the street and someone shoved a cup under my nose, I would throw money in it. If a lady phoned me, requesting that I buy three tacky tea towels for thirty dollars, I would do it. When people came to the office selling stale peanuts, I would think "Yuck" and buy three bags.

Later in the day I would ask myself, "to what cause was I donating?", and I would realize I had no idea! It may be honorable to give to charity, but I wasn't giving out of generosity. I gave mainly because I worried what people thought of me. I didn't want to appear a Scrooge, so I donated. For all I knew, I could have been supporting some terrorist outfit which was about to firebomb my house, but so long as they thought I was nice, I was happy!

Too often I worried about what people thought, instead of considering what I wanted. I never sent back meals in restaurants, wouldn't ask neighbors to turn their music down, rarely returned defective merchandise to a store. When I thought I was being friendly, I was actually being wimpy. My experience is that many people share this preoccupation with the need for approval.

ORIGINS OF THE NEED FOR APPROVAL

As young children we crave approval from our parents, "Look at me! Aren't I clever?" "Do you really like my present?" "Are you proud of me, Dad?"

When we get to school, we survive by getting approval. When the teachers approve of our behavior, we stay out of trouble and get good marks. When teachers don't approve of our views, and our behavior, life can be difficult. We may be allowed some concessional differences during our schooling, but for the most part we depend for success on others' approval of our performance. Into our teen years, we continue to operate on the permission principle – "Is it OK to do this?", ""Can I do that?"

Demands that we conform come from other sources. Many organizations and clubs have harsh rules to keep members in line. "Members are strictly forbidden . . ." Television spreads a similar gospel – "you had better wear the right deodorant, drive the right car, and freshen your breath with 'Clear-o-smell' or everyone will be disgusted with you."

By the time we reach adulthood, we have been heavily conditioned to seek approval. When people condone our behavior, we're happy. But if we don't get the approval we want, we are miserable. This creates a major problem – others are now in control of our happiness!

To take control of our lives, and live fully, our challenge is to eliminate the compulsion to have approval. Ultimately we will either a) have peace of mind or b) worry about what other people think. We can't do both.

Worrying about what others think of us is a tough habit to break, but there can be tragic results if we don't break it. Often, sensible people sentence themselves to a lifetime at jobs they hate, reasoning, "What would people say if I left this secure position?" Mothers confide, "All my life I've wanted to . . . but what would my children say?" Children labor through years of university study to please their parents . . . "I hate everything about this wretched course, but if I quit my parents would go bananas."

It is sad, because our greatest experiences and achievements mostly come from stepping outside our comfort zones and from doing what the masses don't do.

DO YOU WORRY WHAT OTHERS THINK? ASK YOURSELF –

"When was the last time I got poor service in a restaurant, yet said nothing?"

"Do I ever accept invitations because I worry about what they'll think if I say no?"

If you're single – "Do I ever spot someone whom I find attractive, and fail to ask them for a date?"

"Am I always happy to negotiate for what I want? If not, why not?"

"Do I ever buy things I don't want due to pressure from salespeople?"

"If I didn't care what people thought, would I work in the same job, live in the same house with the same people that I do now?"

You can't please even most of the people all of the time. If your fear is that some people might think you're foolish – Relax! They probably already do!

Your family, friends and colleagues no doubt deserve your love and consideration. But when you try to please everyone, you are true to no one, least of all yourself. Peace of mind stems from understanding and accepting that few people will see the world as you see it.

At four years of age, it's important to please people. If others like us, they give us what we want. But things change. When you are forty-five, you need to be an effective human being. You can get what you want by being yourself. You don't have to please everybody. In fact, not only do you not have to, but if you are still trying to please everybody, part of you is still four years old.

IN A NUTSHELL

While respecting others, be true to yourself. If people disagree with your ideas or your lifestyle, it's their business, not yours.

STOP EXPLAINING YOUR LIFE

"TO BE GREAT IS TO BE MISUNDERSTOOD."
— Emerson.

Question. Do you often find yourself justifying your actions? Are you regularly explaining yourself to people?

You'll notice something about confident, self-determined individuals. They don't spend their lives explaining themselves. They just do what they do.

When we're kids, there is no way around it. We are always explaining ourselves to parents and teachers, usually trying to stay out of trouble or

avoiding a spanking. But if we want to be happy adults, we need to think and behave more independently – to be COMFORTABLE ABOUT NOT HAVING TO EXPLAIN OUR EVERY MOVE TO FAMILY, FRIENDS AND NEIGHBORS.

Obviously, sometimes it is appropriate to explain to our boss or justify our actions to our partners. If someone is paying your wages, he has a right to know what you're doing and why you're doing it. In building a close relationship with your life partner, you may often want to share your reasons and ideas. But beyond that, we can recognize that we don't have to go through life as if we are on the witness stand! I'm talking here about personal conviction – about you deciding what is your business and no-one else's. Some people have the habit of asking about things which have nothing to do with them.

When your neighbor says, "Why are you selling your house?", you may prefer to say, "I want to," rather than launch into a great explanation of market trends and your personal finances.

You don't have to be secretive with people. But just because a person asks you a question doesn't mean that it is their business or that you have to answer it to THEIR SATISFACTION.

When your local car salesman invites you to the showroom, and you decline, you don't have to explain anything. He says, "Come and see our latest model. It will blow your socks off." You say, "No, thank you."

"Why not?"

"I have other things in mind. Thanks for the call."

"Yeah, but this car is dynamite. Why don't you want to?"

"I appreciate your thinking of me, but no, thank you." End of conversation.

Consider whether you currently justify your actions and explain things to people which are none of their business. People are not wrong for asking. But you DECIDE TO CONTROL THE SITUATION and answer only the questions which YOU want to.

When your brother-in-law demands, "Why did you quit your job?" you smile and say, "I felt like it."

Your neighbor asks, "Why do you go to the gym six times a week?" You say, "It feels good."

Someone asks, "Will you donate to the 'SAVE THE SNAIL' fund?"

You say "No." You don't have to say, "I'm short of money today," or "I baked a cake for them last week," you just say, "No." No explanation is necessary.

Sometimes people will demand that you explain yourself. They say, "But I don't understand!"

So you say, "That's fine."

"But I really DON'T understand!"

And you say, "You don't have to."

So they become indignant, demanding that you explain how you could possibly do something that doesn't make sense to them, "But why? How could you?"

"I wanted to."

Aunt Rose asks you over for coffee. You say, "Thank you for thinking of us, but we're in the middle of so many chores at the moment . . ."

"Your sister is coming."

"Yes. And she tells me your cookies are sensational."

"But you won't?"

"We'd like to beg out this time, Aunt Rose."

"Why can't you come for a little while?"

"Aunt Rose, we really appreciate your offer. But we'll have to make it some other time."

When dealing with family and close friends, remember that if they call you, they are at least seeking you out. They wish to do something for you and with you – they thought about you. That's not a nuisance, per se. You will probably choose to be more gentle with friends and relatives than with the used car salesman.

If you wish to make friends, sometimes a studied "No" could sound stilted, and even rude. We can say "no" in a variety of imaginative ways. People will generally get the message if, to their obsessive prying, you say, "Let's not worry about my mother-in-law/car/job/money/first love. Look at those flowers. Aren't they gorgeous?"

Some further questions you don't need to answer include —
1. Why don't you ever see your mother-in-law?
2. Why are you so cautious with money? Money is for spending.
3. Why are you so extravagant with money? Think of a rainy day.
4. Why don't you date Chuck?
5. Why don't you buy yourself a new car?

6. Why do you keep trading in your car?

7. Why did you buy THAT?

8. Do you ever regret not marrying Daisy?

9. Why do you go out with HIM?

10. Is that ALL you're doing?

Be free to live as you choose, doing with your time as you see fit. You don't have to explain your whole life and social calendar to everyone else's satisfaction. You needn't be rude, but be in control of your life. Don't be a victim.

We don't always have to have reasons in life, anyway. If something feels nice, that may be a good enough reason — like taking a bath, singing in the shower, spending a day in bed. Never having done something before may also be a good enough reason to do it — and it is your business.

IN A NUTSHELL

Make your own decisions. Don't set out to offend people, but be true to yourself. IF YOU CHOOSE TO EXPLAIN YOURSELF, DO IT BECAUSE YOU WANT TO SHARE YOUR THOUGHTS WITH ANOTHER PERSON AND NOT BECAUSE YOU NEED THEIR APPROVAL. Your own permission is sufficient — you don't need other people's.

WHEN YOU WANT TO SAY "NO"

Isn't it sometimes difficult to say no? How often have you found yourself giving up a precious Saturday afternoon, buying a silly subscription, accepting a dinner invitation, joining a committee, lending someone money, just because you could not say "NO!"

For our own mental health and happiness, we must be able to say "No!" when it suits us – AND NOT FEEL GUILTY. Saying "Yes" when we mean "No" leads to anger, depression and resentment. WE ARE HAPPY IN LIFE TO THE EXTENT THAT WE BELIEVE WE HAVE CONTROL OVER OUR CIRCUMSTANCES, AND TAKING CONTROL OF OUR LIVES OFTEN MEANS SAYING – "No."

(We should also understand that when other people say "No", they have their reasons.)

GUILT MANIPULATION

Why is it tough to say "No"? Sometimes we fear that if we assert ourselves, people won't like us. Sometimes we allow ourselves to feel guilty, (with other people's encouragement), and the moment we feel guilty, they know we'll do all kinds of things to rid ourselves of the guilt.

Let's look at some simple examples of how others encourage us to feel guilty –

Mother says, "I've been feeling ill all morning. Would you stop what you are doing and go to the supermarket for me?"

(Message: I'm sick so if you don't do what I want, you are a very uncaring person).

Boyfriend says, "If you really love me you will sleep with me."

(Message: If you don't do what I WANT, that means you want to hurt my feelings – so feel guilty).

Boss says, "I'm going to be working until ten o'clock tonight. I need you to stay back late."

(Message: I've decided to work my head off, so you had better do the same).

An old friend says, "You must come out for a drink – after all, we are old friends."

(Message: if you don't do what I WANT, you are not being a good friend).

Your mechanic says, "We have worked on this car of yours day and

night. We have done our best, and you can't ask for more."

(Message: Don't be unreasonable and expect us to fix this heap. Just pay us the two thousand for repairs and tow it away).

In each of these cases, the other person is making or implying a judgment as to what you "should" do. They are making a decision as to what is morally correct . . . "if you are a good person, you will shop for me, sleep with me, see me on the weekend, not complain that I wrecked your car . . ." etc.

BE YOUR OWN JUDGE

The only way to escape guilt manipulation by others is to be your own judge. Refuse to be tied to their view of right and wrong. Make up your own mind, and be prepared to voice it. You then say to your mother, "Perhaps the shopping could wait a little while, Mom? This is very important." You say to your boyfriend, "I appreciate that you believe I should sleep with you. My view is . . ."

Some people are very persistent in their requests.

You say, "No."

They say, "Why not?"

You say, "I don't want to."

They say, "Why not?"

You say, "I have other things to do."

They say, "What about our friendship?"

You say, "It has nothing to do with our friendship."

They say, "If you don't, it means you don't care."

And so finally you say, "OK , I'll do it."

(Guilt manipulation wins again).

A lot of salesmen know about manipulation. A salesman arrives at your door and engages you in conversation –

Salesman - "Do you have a minute?"

You - "What for?"

Salesman - "I'm doing a survey – I'd like your help."

You - "On what?"

Salesman - "Education."

You - "You aren't selling anything, are you?"

Salesman - "Not exactly."

You - "What are those twenty six volumes labelled A to Z that you have under your left arm?"

Salesman - "Oh, just books."

You - "They look suspiciously like encyclopedias to me."

Salesman - "They do, don't they?"

You - "Before you go any further, I do not want to buy any encyclopedias."

Salesman - "Fine. May I ask you one question?"

You - "Err. .. OK."

Salesman - "Do you have children?"

You - "Yes, two."

Salesman - "Are you interested in their education?"

You - "Err... yes." (Now you have answered two questions).

Salesman - "You would be keen to see them enjoy advantages that you never had, wouldn't you?"

You - "I guess so."

Salesman - "Are you hoping that they'll make a success of their lives?"

You - "Yes."

Salesman - "So you are keen to help them with their education?"

You - "Err... yes but ..."

Salesman - "You really care about those kids of yours, don't you?"

(Message: "If you really care about those dear little children of yours, you'll spend your life savings on my encyclopedias").

Fifteen minutes later:

Salesman - "You won't be sorry. You are now the proud owner of the full 26 volume set of Cosmic Encyclopedias — and luckily for you, I happen to have a set right here under my left arm!"

You now have two thousand dollars worth of books you don't want, and you're wondering how in the heck you bought them. To get what you want, you have to be more persistent than the other person. If they ask you four times, you be prepared to say "No" five times. If they ask you ten times, you say "No" eleven.

One of the best ways to do this is with the "Broken Record" technique. The great thing about this approach is that to use it effectively, you don't need to be a great arguer or debater. You stick with one principle – STATE WHAT YOU WANT AND DON"T GET SIDETRACKED. Don't be manipulated, don't answer questions, just state what you want.

Here's how you would apply the "BROKEN RECORD" approach to our book vendor —

You - "You aren't selling anything, are you?"

Salesman - "Not exactly."

You - "Are you selling encyclopedias?"

Salesman - "Well . . .yes."

You - "Before we go any further, I DON'T WANT TO BUY ANY ENCYCLOPEDIAS."

Salesman - "May I ask you one question?"

You - "I DON'T WANT TO BUY ANY ENCYCLOPEDIAS."

Salesman - "You look like a person who is interested in world events."

You - "I might look that way, and I DON'T WANT TO BUY ANY ENCYCLOPEDIAS."

Salesman - "Do you have children?"

You - "I DON'T WANT TO BUY ANY ENCYCLOPEDIAS."

Salesman - "But how can you say "No" when you haven't even seen my encyclopedias? They could be a real bargain!"

You - "I'm sure they could be, but I DON'T WANT TO BUY ANY ENCYCLOPEDIAS."

Salesman - "These are the best value encyclopedias on the market today. It will take two minutes . . ."

You - "I'm sure you believe they're the best value, I guess it would take two minutes and I DON'T WANT TO BUY ANY ENCYCLOPEDIAS."

Salesman - "I've had a terrible week."

You - "I empathize with you - AND I DON'T WANT TO BUY ANY ENCYCLOPEDIAS."

Salesman - "If I don't sell some of these encyclopedias by lunch time, my boss will shoot me!"

You - "I'm sure he will shoot you, and I DON'T WANT TO BUY ANY ENCYCLOPEDIAS."

Salesman - "You don't even care that my seventeen children will starve!"

You - "I bet it seems I don't care, and I DON'T WANT TO BUY ANY ENCYCLOPEDIAS."

Chances are that you can think of other ways of dealing with door-to-door salesmen — like slamming doors in their faces. However, we are looking at a method which is valuable in many situations where you find yourself being pushed around. It might be a good idea to practice on these guys so that you refine your skills for times when you cannot "escape" by just slamming the front door.

When using the BROKEN RECORD, remember the following —

a) Don't get too excited. Keep your voice in a monotone, be cool and authoritative.

b) Your aim is not to offend the other party. Unless you like hurling and receiving abuse, agree with them where possible. eg. "I'm sure they are a bargain...I probably do seem uncaring...it must appear that way to you ...BUT I DON'T WANT TO BUY ANY ENCYCLOPEDIAS."

c) USE THE SAME WORDS. Your impact will be much stronger if you use exactly the same words each time you state your case.

d) BE PERSISTENT. When you have a strategy like the BROKEN RECORD, you can really start to make a game of it — and play to win.

COUNTERING MANIPULATION WITH QUESTIONS

When the BROKEN RECORD isn't appropriate, one or two incisive questions can often let another person know that you won't be pushed around.

An acquaintance says, "If you were any kind of friend you would lend me a thousand dollars."

QUESTION. "Why would a friend necessarily lend you a thousand dollars?"

"Because I need it."

QUESTION. "I'm sure you do. Are you saying that I'm no friend if I fail to lend you money?"

"Well . . . no."

"I just wanted to get that straight. I consider myself a friend of yours, but I don't have a thousand to spare right now."

Wife says, "If you cared about me, you wouldn't spend the whole weekend fishing."

QUESTION. "What is it about my going fishing that bugs you?"

"When you are fishing, I don't see you."

QUESTION. "You miss me?"

"Yes I do."

QUESTION. "Isn't it good that we still miss each other?"

"I suppose so."

QUESTION. "I want to go fishing, but let's also plan some time together later in the week. How would that be?"

"That would be OK"

BROKEN RECORD and QUESTIONING strategies are valuable firstly because they can give you greater confidence in situations where previously you felt nervous or out of control. To successfully say "No", you must be able to hold a different view and not feel guilty for it.

Although at times others may seek to influence our behavior with guilt manipulation, more often there is no manipulation on their part — they are simply making a request and our challenge is to be comfortable about standing up for what we want.

Drawing the line between assertiveness and selfishness is tricky, and no doubt you will often be told, "You are being selfish!" when you believe you are being assertive.

IN A NUTSHELL

Be your own judge as to what is fair, and don't allow others to sentence you to weeks or years of guilt based on their perceptions of right and wrong. With your own family especially, you need to be able to say "No." Once you can say "NO" without guilt, you take greater control of your life, and you can live more happily with other people as well as yourself.

OTHER PEOPLE'S EXPECTATIONS

Remember that people like strength and expect respect. They also need space.

THE VALUE OF COMPLIMENTS

Show me someone who says he or she doesn't want to feel important and I'll show you a liar.

We all need recognition and praise. Our appetite for praise is like our appetite for food — it is never satisfied for long. Surveys in the work place show that in the hierarchy of people's wants, money is well down the list. Needs like "recognition by the company", "praise when it's due" and "making a contribution" consistently rank before cash reward.

Even the rich and famous like to be told regularly that they are looking good and doing well. Watch interviews with movie stars, sports stars and business tycoons, and you'll notice that they lap up genuine praise as eagerly as the next person.

Ask yourself, "AM I TOLD THAT I AM BEAUTIFUL, CLEVER, CAPABLE, EFFICIENT, LOVEABLE AND WONDERFUL AS OFTEN AS I WOULD LIKE?" The answer is "NO," isn't it? The same goes for everyone else in the world. We never get enough.

You probably know the conclusion I'll draw here — If you want TO INFLUENCE OTHERS, COMPLIMENT THEM! You don't have to be a toady. Neither must you heap upon them litanies of insincere or obviously false compliments. Simply recognize their good points and let them know. They will remember you.

My friend Peter delivered his car to a repair shop. On driving the car into the garage, he insisted on seeing the owner. The owner arrived, no doubt wondering what he had done wrong, where upon Peter said, "I wanted to see you personally just to tell you that this is the most beautiful service area I have ever seen. It is so clean and organized. It is a joy to come here and it is a credit to you."

The man was bowled over. For twenty years he had been putting his heart and soul into maintaining his garage and nobody had ever told him it was beautiful.

Sometimes you may compliment people and they'll be awkward or embarrassed. But be assured that inside they'll be glowing. I am stunned that so many beautiful women receive such few compliments. Frequently I have said, "You have such a pretty face," or "Do a lot of people comment on your lovely eyes?" and they look at me in disbelief. Everyone thinks they know that they are lovely, so no one ever tells them.

WHY PRAISE ALWAYS WORKS

On the surface, others may look very confident, self assured and happy with themselves, but when you are talking to a successful, good looking, impressive person, he doesn't see himself exactly in those terms. He deals with his inner self, which is sometimes nervous, often worried, maybe disorganized He knows that part of himself that never felt good enough, that part of himself which says, "I wish I had blue eyes, was an inch taller, and hadn't made so many mistakes in my life."

Therefore, when you say something to this fellow which to you seems obvious, like, "You're very successful. You should be very proud of your achievements," it comes as a breath of fresh air. He'll be over the moon.

SECOND HAND PRAISE

Another option for praising others is second hand praise – telling a person the good things that you've heard about them. People are always delighted to learn that their friends and relatives speak well of them.

Second hand praise is also effective when you are buying someone's services for the first time. If you are needing the services of a doctor, a printer, a mechanic, a gardener, chances are you will ask a friend to recommend somebody.

Assuming that you have a recommendation, a good way to start a friendship and to ensure excellent service is to tell them you've heard fine reports . . .

"Bob tells me you're the best mechanic around . . ."

"My boss says that you know more about these machines than anybody. . ."

"Your mother tells me you're the best doctor in the country. . ."

Firstly, they will appreciate the recognition, and secondly, they'll want to live up to the reputation.

IN A NUTSHELL

People crave recognition. If you will choose to see their good points, and give compliments where possible, they'll feel wonderful, and you'll get a kick too.

TEDDY

The deputy principal at my elementary school was a man named Edward Gare He stood about five feet tall. He had a round body and a round red face. Everyone knew him as Teddy Bear.

He taught seventh grade, and strange things would happen to the children in Teddy's class. They would start to work. I mean really work! Eleven year old children would spend four and five hours a night studying because they WANTED to! It was a phenomenon. I experienced a year of Teddy's magic and learned something of how he produced his extraordinary results. But to those whom Teddy never taught, it seemed like he cast a spell on his students.

He was not an entertaining teacher. He wasn't a barrel of laughs and he was no great academic. But Teddy knew how to praise kids, he knew how to encourage us, he knew how to care. Teddy used to give us little merit cards for effort, merit cards for good work, gold stars, stamps. He took time for us. He wouldn't just give a mark of an "A" or a "B". He would write his own "essays" at the bottom of our essays, telling us where we had done well and where we could improve.

Many of the children who spent a year with Teddy felt real praise for the first time. Teddy touched all of us – even the roughest and the toughest.

I remember my brother Christopher announcing that if he ever became one of Teddy's class, he wasn't going to do a scrap of anything. He told us, "No way am I going to crawl to Teddy!" As fate would have it, Chris did become Teddy's student. He was soon spending six hours a night on his homework, and by the end of the year he'd earned more merit cards than any pupil in the school's history.

Teddy's results were a continuing affirmation of the power of praise. He got results because he really cared – he loved those kids – and he would always find some good somewhere.

TALKING

Your task in life is not necessarily to get everyone to like you. But if you are going to spend your life meeting people at parties, dinner, work, school, at the local supermarket, it makes sense to know how to talk to others easily.

People feel comfortable with you if they feel that you are a bit like them – if you have things in common. If they can identify with you and sense that you understand them, if they can get a peek at your humanity – they will be happy talking to you.

We can learn a lot about communication by observing public speakers. Firstly, think of the WORST speakers you have ever heard, and of how they so skillfully lost their audience . . .

Fred Nerd rises to his feet to address the multitude. He begins, "It gives me great pleasure to be here . . ." (You say to yourself, Oh no! Those same old clichés).

"Unaccustomed as I am to public speaking, I eerrr umm...I'll try not to bore you." (Even he admits he's bad!).

"When I think back over my long career . . ." (Now he is going to talk about himself!)

"I was born in 1923 . . ." (Oh no! We are getting his whole life story!)

"My family at that time . . ." (And his family history!)

An hour later,". . . I see that I have little time left . . ." (God save us!).

". . . so in this last half hour . . ." (OH NO! Somebody do something! A bullet perhaps?)

"...I want to talk about myself..." (I can't stand it! I'm leaving).

These characters bore us to tears. They don't identify with us, they talk too much about themselves, they rarely laugh at themselves, and they're so worried about the impression they're creating, they're afraid to be honest and original.

Good speakers do the exact opposite. They relate to their audience in terms of common interests, experiences and fears. Good speakers are so busy being themselves that they give little thought to the impression they're making, and they are able to see the funny side of things.

The same rules apply when talking to one person as when talking to a thousand. You don't have to dazzle them with your intellect and wit. If you a) FIND THINGS IN COMMON, b) CARE and c) BE HUMAN you'll chat quite easily with almost everyone.

FINDING THINGS IN COMMON

Whenever you meet somebody new, they are wondering if you are like them. Your challenge is to discover your similarities.

People who turn others off, are always finding differences. Their message is, "I'm richer than you. I'm more successful than you. I'm more interesting than you. My car is better than your heap. I don't even want to talk about you. I disagree with everything you say anyway..."

Conversations with these people go like this –

You say, "The salmon paté is beautiful."

They say, "Salmon gives me hives."

You say, "I am going to France this summer."

They say, "My dog died in France."

You say, " I'm going skiing on the weekend."

They say, "I broke my leg skiing."

You walk away thinking, "Why would anyone ever want to talk to that person?"

Striking a common note with people is a skill you develop like any other. Often it means finding the simple things. It means making the effort to share something of yourself and being aware enough to uncover common interests.

CARING

Think of the last time you had a conversation with someone, and you had the impression that they really weren't that interested in talking to you. Did you feel irritated? We need to remind ourselves that other people can also tell when we are not that interested in them.

To attract others we have to care about them. When we are vitally interested in someone, there is rarely a problem in keeping the conversation going. When we care, we forget about ourselves. We stop wondering, "What am I going to say next?" There are no more of those long, uneasy silences during which you both look around the room, check your watch and agree again that the weather has been very nice. Caring means putting ourselves in the other person's shoes – setting aside our own experiences and saying, "You tell me your story."

If you don't want to make the effort to care, it is probably better to leave! Find some company you really want, take a bath, read a book, rather than spend an evening going through the motions with people you don't want to be with. If you are going to talk to people, why not give them your whole attention?

LISTENING

Speaking of attention, let's talk about listening. Ninety-eight percent of people are desperate for someone to really listen to them. Next time you are talking to someone, take note of whether they really listen to you. Do they absorb every word you say, or do they continually look over your shoulder, glance at their watch, jangle their money, study the drapes?

Do they ever repeat what they think you have said, just to check that they understand, or are they just waiting for you to shut your mouth so that they can talk?

As sure as we need food and drink, so do we need friends who will truly listen. Seneca's words, of 4 BC. ring as true for us today as they did two thousand years ago –

"Listen to me for a day, an hour, a moment
Lest I expire in my terrible wilderness, my
lonely silence! Oh God, is there no one to listen?"

I have had the privilege of conducting one particular listening exercise with hundreds of people in my seminars. It goes like this: the exercise is done in pairs, with a person A and a person B. Person A gets to talk for 3 minutes while person B listens intently. While person A is talking, person B is not allowed to say ANYTHING. No interruption, no "Yeah. Me too's." No scratching, just pure listening. There is gentle eye-to-eye contact throughout the exercise.

At the end of the first 3 minutes, roles are reversed. Person B talks and person A listens intently. Each person gets to talk 4 times and listen 4 times.

This would seem a simple exercise on paper, yet the participants' reactions have never ceased to amaze me. Most people remark, "I have never ever been listened to like that in my life!" Countless married couples have told me, "We haven't listened to each other like this in 30 years!"

Complete strangers jokingly announce, "We're in love!" After just twenty five minutes of listening.

Think about it. Don't you like it when someone gives you his total attention? Isn't it a special experience to have another take the trouble to see life through your eyes? Well, the next person that you speak to will no doubt feel the same. People out there are starving for someone to listen TOTALLY. If you would choose to affect people positively, try listening with 100 percent of your attention. You will become a special person for them.

LISTENING WITHOUT JUDGING

Speak to any partner in a failing relationship and they'll make remarks like "We just don't talk anymore . . .", "There's no communication in the marriage . . .", "My father just won't listen to me . . ."

The recurrent theme is again LISTENING. With loved ones it is so crucial: not only that we listen but that we listen without judging. We are all so vulnerable. We need at least one person with whom we can share our deepest concerns – one person who will say, "I love and accept you as you are, no matter what." If we fear that when we expose our feelings, they'll say, "You're disgusting!" or "Shame on you!", we'll share nothing and gradually we'll drift apart. Many times there is no need for the listener to express an opinion. Just to be able to share our feelings with a sympathetic human being is enough.

DO WHAT YOU SAY

It is said that people can be divided into three groups. "A few people make it happen, a lot of people watch it happen, and the rest don't even know what happened!"

Here's part of the formula for membership of the first group – Do what you say you'll do! Most people don't. They say they'll do all kinds of things and don't deliver.

How often do you hear others say, "I'll call you" and they don't, say "I'm going to get fit," and they get fatter, say "I'll help you if I can," when you know they won't? How often do people say "I'll pay my bill," and you never see them again?

When we begin to take our word seriously, a number of things happen:

- Others trust us.
- We consider very carefully before we commit ourselves.
- We become more honest with others.
- We are better able to avoid unwanted situations.
- We get to like ourselves better.

When you take no notice of what you say, other people take no notice of you. If you don't believe yourself, other people don't believe you either. You can generally sense lack of commitment in other people, which means the reverse is generally true. People sense what stuff you're made of.

So how do you become a person of your word? YOU MAKE CHOICES, ADMIT TO THEM AND STICK TO THEM.

When the neighbors invite you over for drinks, and you think to yourself, "I'd rather die than go there!" don't say, "Sounds great! I really hope I can make it." Instead, be honest. You might say, "Thank you for thinking of me, but I won't be there this afternoon."

In this, and similar situations, be tactful, respect your own wishes, state your case and don't feel guilty for being true to yourself.

For those times when you don't know what you'll do or where you'll be, don't promise anything. Be straight. A lot of people live in fairy land, never thinking things through, and never asking themselves the tough questions like, "How am I going to pay for this?" or "Am I a hundred percent committed?"

For those times when people ask for your commitment, and you are genuinely unsure about whether you can help, don't make promises. The best approach is to say, "I don't know yet, but if I'm coming, I'll phone you." Far better to deal with it this way, and to call them later with the good news, ("I'll be there"), than to say "I'll be there!" and then have to phone them later with the bad news.

PEOPLE WANT TO SEE STRENGTH

People love to see strength. Even though sometimes they may test you, they're often hoping to find someone who has conviction. Your neighbors, your friends, your colleagues want you to be strong – so many people are like leaves in the breeze.

When you launch into your new diet plan, and they tempt you with cream cakes, they're secretly hoping that you'll stick with it.

Children especially need to admire strong people – people who will make a promise or a threat and keep to it. Draw a line and your child will walk over it. He's just testing to see who is stronger – and hoping that you are.

It's a very uneasy feeling for children to believe that they're in control and can do anything they want. They desperately need someone to make some rules and enforce them. Sometimes they'll swear, curse, break things, shout, scream, steal and run away, just hoping that someone will give them some boundaries.

People admire you when you make a stand, though they might not agree with the cause.

IN A NUTSHELL

Every time you say that you'll do something, and end up doing something totally different, you're chipping away at your personal power. Certainly it is fine to change our mind sometimes. But for the most part, we need to be demonstrating to ourselves that we are in control of our lives by keeping to our word.

The more you stand by your commitments, the stronger you become.

To influence others, you must believe in yourself. To believe in yourself, you must believe what you say, and do what you say.

PEOPLE WANT RESPECT

Sometimes we deal with shopkeepers, neighbors, in-laws (and husbands and wives) who give us trouble. Despite our most earnest attempts to get along with them, they seem hopelessly unreasonable!

This chapter shares some strategies on how you can avoid arguments and get people on your side. If you genuinely enjoy confrontations, skip this bit – or read it and do the opposite!

Imagine yourself in the following situations . . .

• You are wheeling your groceries to the supermarket checkout. Just as you are about to reach the counter, a woman with a full cart hurtles past you without so much as an apology or an "excuse me."

Consequently, you are delayed by about two minutes. Most likely you will feel a little angry – but are you angry over the lost two minutes or over her lack of consideration?

• You're at a party. Someone you have known for years notices you but doesn't bother to say "Hello". Again, you may feel irritated. Why?

• While being served your salad at a restaurant, you notice that the lettuce is brown around the edges. You draw the waiter's attention to the state of the lettuce whereupon he suggests, "Just cut the bad edges off – they won't kill you!" If you feel angry, is it because you're losing a mouthful of salad?"

It's not the two-minute delay nor the "Hello" or the lost pieces of lettuce that really worry us. It's the treatment we receive. MOST TIMES WHEN WE GET ANGRY, IT'S NOT FOR THE REASON WE THINK. We get angry, when we feel others don't care about us. We want respect. EVERYONE WANTS RESPECT.

WE ALL MAKE THE SAME MISTAKE...

It may seem obvious that everyone wants respect – and most of us know it. The trouble starts when we get into an argument. Then we begin to list all the EXCUSES for why we did what we did, and forget to show respect for the other person.

Imagine that your partner has called you and specifically asked you to pick up the dry cleaning on the way home from work. The facts are –

a) your partner usually picks up the dry cleaning

b) your partner is easily upset

c) you arrive home without the dry cleaning

d) your partner gets upset

Don't be fooled. Your partner is probably far more concerned that you should care, concerned about your wavering desire to help out, than he or she is actually miffed by the lack of dry cleaning. This being so, the following list of excuses or reactions won't help your relationship –

a) "I had enough to worry about without your dry cleaning!"

b) "What a day I've had! Boss problems, car problems, client problems, money problems – and you're worried about some silly dry cleaning!"

c) "I forgot I had to get it."

d) "I forgot I was married."

e) "Damn your dry cleaning!."

All of these remarks have a similar message – "My needs are more important than your needs," and "I'm more important than you!" It's dangerous territory. Your partner immediately decides that "you don't do anything to help", that "you only think of yourself" and most importantly "YOU DON'T CARE." Suddenly you're on the brink of divorce, all over the pointless issue of dry cleaning.

"But", you say, "I really DID have boss problems," or "someone DID steal the wheels off of my car," or "I DID lose my wallet today. THOSE ARE THE

FACTS!" Why is this person being so unreasonable?"

They 're being unreasonable because people don't want FACTS – at least, not at first. They want to know that you CARE! They want your empathy. They want respect. Once they know you care, then maybe they'll listen to the facts, but first they want you to care.

Recall, for example, the brown lettuce salad saga at the restaurant. You don't want facts. You don't need the waiter telling you, "We're too busy to cut off brown edges today," or "Too bad. You got the bum end of the last lettuce." You want respect..."Madam, I can understand that you should feel upset about this. I would be too. Would it be all right if I brought you a new salad?... Is there anything else?" Wouldn't you feel happier with that approach?

How can you show respect? Follow a few simple rules.

1. LISTEN. Nothing brings a person of sound mind to the point of violence more quickly than the feeling that you are not listening to him. Listening indicates respect. Listening makes the others feel important. Have some eye contact when they're explaining how they feel.

2. EMPATHIZE. Let the person know that you can appreciate how he feels ... "You must feel really irritated that the one time you asked me to help out, I let you down! It must seem to you that I couldn't care less."

3. IDENTIFY. Establish common ground – "If the situation were reversed, I would feel just like you," or "I don't blame you for being upset. I would be too."

4. "WHAT ELSE?" When they have had their say, ask them "Is there anything else I should know about?" Irritated people are always happily surprised when you ask, "Is there anything else you want to tell me?" They are so used to having the other party always trying to shut them up. When they sense that you are giving them all the time they want, their aggression evaporates, and they will usually stop attacking right there.

5. "WHAT WOULD YOU LIKE ME TO DO?" When people believe that you don't care, and you ask them, "What do you want me to do?" they'll probably say something like "walk across town and fix it right now" or "find a very tall building and jump out of it."

However, when the irate person feels that you do care, very often all their demands will dissolve. You'll hear, "It's not that important, really," or "I guess I can fix it myself." Try it. It's amazing. One minute they're threatening to sue you for your shirt, and the next minute they're saying "Forget it!"

Recently I shared these principles in a lecture. Some days later I met a fellow from the lecture, George, who had since used these tips.

George had a furniture business, and he had delivered some furniture to a customer that day, two days after his promised delivery date. Out came the purchaser, fuming, and ready for a fight, "How dare you! You said you'd be here two days ago."

George resisted his normal urge to make excuses and simply said, "If I had ordered some furniture and it came two days late, I would be very angry too!" The fellow immediately cooled down. "Well," he said "I guess it could have been worse."

George told me, "It was amazing. "When I made no excuses, and let him know I appreciated his position, his attitude changed instantly. Suddenly I don't fear irate people any more."

Using these principles is easier in theory than in practice. Even when you think you grasp the idea, you will probably want to make excuses when under pressure out of sheer habit. Don't! At least, not until the other person knows you empathize with his position.

SO WHEN CAN I USE EXCUSES?

Sometimes reasons and facts will be appropriate, for example, "The reason I'm late is because someone stole my car," but this should come after the empathy... "Darling, you must feel very upset that I should be two hours late for our wedding." The rule is EMPATHY FIRST, EXCUSES SECOND.

IN A NUTSHELL

In dealing with angry people, FACTS DON'T WORK. CARE AND RESPECT DO WORK. We are not talking about a set of techniques here, so much as a change of attitude. LISTEN, EMPATHIZE and GIVE RESPECT, and ninety-eight percent of people will give you few problems.

TELL PEOPLE HOW YOU FEEL

"I KNOW MY HUSBAND CAN BE LOVING AND KIND – HE'S THAT WAY WITH THE DOG."

A lonely lady made this remark to Leo Buscaglia, and he quoted it in one of his talks on "Love". A little sad isn't it, that a man takes a wife "for richer, for poorer, for better or for worse" and gives his affection to the beagle?"

Often the problem is not that we don't care, but that we don't know how to show we care. Sometimes it's awkward and embarrassing so we wait and we say nothing. We tell ourselves, "One day I'll really tell my mother how much I love her." Sometimes we wait until it is too late.

I have a friend, Paul, who, age 33, decided he was going to tell his father how much he loved him. They had had a rocky relationship and it is wonderful to hear Paul tell the story. . .

"I wanted to tell Dad that I really appreciated all that he had done for me over the years. I wanted him to know that I appreciated how he'd picked me up from scouts, and appreciated how he always watched me play football and how he worked at two jobs to put me through college. I wanted to tell him that despite everything, I cared for him.

"He only lived fifty miles away but I was too scared to tell him to his face. I was too chicken even to tell him on the phone. So I decided to write him a letter . . . "Dear Dad, I know that we have had some problems lately. We haven't talked for five years . . ." and I went on to say how, despite our differences, I loved and admired him so much. I told him all the things that I couldn't say to his face and I sent the letter off.

"A couple of days later I got a phone call. It was my father – "Paul, it's Dad. We got your letter. Here's Mom." The conversation was short but it was a start!

"A few weeks after that, I decided to drive up and watch my father play tennis at his club. He had spent years watching me play my sport, so I thought I would watch him. After the match he took me into the clubhouse to meet some of his friends. He introduced me to the nearest fellow, and this guy said, "Paul! You're the one who wrote the letter!" The next fellow I was introduced to said, "Pleased to meet you. You must be the one who wrote the letter!" Guess what the next guy said – "You must be the one who wrote that letter." There were about 300 people at that club and it seemed that everyone knew about the letter I sent to my Dad. Maybe he'd stuck it on the message board or put it in the bulletin! One man said to me, "I'm worth two million dollars and I would give every penny of it to have a letter like that from my son."

Paul says, "Dad and I started spending weekends together, going on vacations to the snow, our whole relationship has changed. It used to be I couldn't talk to him. Now, every time I see him I get a bear hug.

Whenever we admit to our feelings and tell people we care, we risk. It takes courage. Like most risk taking, there can be great rewards. Our loved ones need to be told. They want to be reassured. One fellow asked, "When is the best time to tell your wife that you love her?" The answer is, "Before someone else does."

Jim Rohn points out, "Words are no substitute for action, but the reverse is also true. ACTION IS NO SUBSTITUTE FOR WORDS." Frank works eighty hours a week to feed and clothe his family and says, "They should KNOW that I love them! Look how hard I work! Surely I don't have to TELL them as well!" Yes, Frank, you do have to tell them. They probably don't know.

May says, "Mother should know that I appreciate her." Well, perhaps she should, but she probably doesn't. People aren't mind readers. By all means stroke the dog, but stroke your loved ones as well. The same things work for people as work with dogs! Praise them often, give them a pat on the back, hug them, tell them you love them. Dogs can never get enough of that stuff. Neither can your wife ... or husband ... or lover ... as the case may be.

87

IN A NUTSHELL

Though we think that others know how much we care, they usually don't. Sometimes we are so busy demonstrating that we love them that we forget to TELL them. We all want to be told — OFTEN.

"I WANT TO TELL THEM BUT I DON'T KNOW HOW"

You must know people who have said, "I want to tell them I care but I would be too embarrassed. I wouldn't know what to say or how to put it. They might think I was stupid." In case you're one of those people, you might want to use the following paragraph. It is for you to show to someone whom you care about . . .

TO YOU FROM ME

I'm hoping you'll read this paragraph. I'm reading this chapter on "telling people that you care about them," and it relates to you and me. I'm one of those people who find it hard to say "I love you." I guess I always assume you know it, and that I don't need to say it. I also don't want to sound awkward or be embarrassed, so I tend to avoid telling you how I really feel. The truth is that I love you so much, and feel very lucky to have you in my life. Maybe this little announcement is unexpected. Perhaps you're surprised to be getting it from a book! Now that I've told you this way, I hope I'll be able to tell you "I LOVE YOU" more often. I just wanted you to know. Now you can return my book.

PEOPLE NEED SPACE

"Sing and dance and be joyous,
but let each one also be alone.
Even as the strings of the lute are alone,
though they quiver to the same music."
— *Kahlil Gibran.*

No matter how much people love you, sometimes they want you to just leave them alone.

Sometimes we can forget that we are each individuals who need our own space, and when our partner decides to do something for themselves, by themselves, we feel rejected . . .

Fred says to Mary, "I'm going fishing."

Mary asks, "By YOURSELF?"

Fred, "Yes, sometimes I enjoy being alone."

"Why? What have I done?" Mary is hurt.

"Nothing. I just like the solitude."

"Well, can't I come and enjoy the solitude with you?"

"Mary! I just want to go by myself."

"But I'm your wife!"

"Yes, and I love you, and I'm also going fishing."

"If you loved me you'd want to take ME fishing."

"Give me a break, Mary!"

"I've done something wrong, and you're not telling me!"

"You've done nothing wrong. I just need some space every now and then."

"I think you're trying to get away from me."

"No, really. . ."

If Mary keeps this up, Fred soon will be going fishing just to get away from her!

Most of us need time alone to clear our heads, to process thoughts, to formulate strategies, to be with nature, to get things in perspective. Sometimes we just need to be alone so that we can miss someone, and fall in love with them all over again.

If you live with a person seven days a week, at some stage they will probably start to drive you crazy. . . they forget to pick up your dry cleaning for the third time in a week, they spend the whole morning on the telephone, you find their toenail clippings on the edge of the sink again, and that's when you really know you need some space.

IN A NUTSHELL

We need to be sensitive to others' needs. SOMETIMES THE BEST WAY TO GET ALONG WITH SOMEONE IS TO BE ABSENT!

CHAPTER 5

LIVING (MORE EASILY) WITH OTHERS

It's What You Don't Say

Taking Offense

Avoiding Arguments

Telling People "You're Wrong"

Humiliating People

Criticism

Ask Questions First!

Anger Doesn't Motivate

Establish The Rules

Learning From Mistakes

You Get What You Expect

Form Wins Friends

Expectations In A Friendship

Limits Of Friendship

Many times, others appreciate us more for what we don't say.

IT'S WHAT YOU DON'T SAY...

"DRAWING ON MY FINE COMMAND OF LANGUAGE, I SAID NOTHING."

— Robert Benchley

Angela is given a diamond ring by her husband. She's touched. It's a romantic moment. She looks deep into his eyes and says, "Darling, it's beautiful. I love it! I'll treasure it always!" Returning her gaze he replies, "You had better! It cost me a damn fortune!"

Aren't some things better left unsaid? One of life's important lessons can be learning when to keep our mouth shut. If your comment isn't going to fix anything or make anyone feel better, it's best to scrap it.

SOME THINGS OTHER PEOPLE JUST DON'T WANT TO HEAR! Others don't want to hear you grousing about your husband. They don't want to hear about your aching back or your stuffy nose or how overdrawn you are or how many times you went to the bathroom last night.

Next time you're about to complain about something, ask yourself, "Why would anyone want to hear this?"

How would you feel about a James Bond who constantly moaned about his cold sores? What if Superman whined about the weather and the price of detergent? Wouldn't he lose a little of his charisma? The same applies to us. We admire special people who can smile when things are tough. We appreciate those who handle disappointment without throwing tantrums.

It doesn't matter how many degrees you have or whether you wear designer clothes, and live in the ritzy suburbs, if you are a complainer, you have no style. If you ever want to make an impression on someone – for example, a boss or a boyfriend – wait for a disaster and then handle it without complaint. You will be noticed! – so few people do it. They will be impressed by your strength and they'll want you on their team.

On bitching and complaining, here is an abbreviated list of things people don't want to hear . . .

a) "I've got a headache."

b) "My husband snored all night."

c) "I'm broke."

d) "Life isn't fair. People are always nasty to me."

e) "My bunions are giving me trouble again."

f) "Your birthday present cost me a fortune."

g) "I'm in a terrible mood."

h) "I hate myself, I'm ugly, I'm boring . . ."

i) "I've got the flu, and you'll get it too."

j) "The world is going to end on Friday."

People also resent "You should have's". Don't you hate it when someone gives you advice you didn't ask for, when it's too late to do anything anyway?

You buy yourself a suit at Bozo's Boutique, and you tell your brother, "Isn't it great? Only $499!" That's when he says, "Too bad. I could have gotten you one of those for two hundred bucks.

I have a friend who, when I call her on the telephone, grumbles about the fact that I never call her . . . "Why don't you ever call me? Do you know how long it's been? You never call me. Why is it that you don't call me?" Guess why I don't call her.

To add to the list of "You should have's" that people don't need . . .

a) "You should have done it this way"

b) "You should have sold your house last week/ last year"

c) "You should have been here yesterday."

d) "You should be like me and get a job, lose weight, stop smoking, go to church . . ."

e) "You should have told me."

f) "You should be ashamed of yourself."

My father always knew what to leave unsaid. I remember, when I was eighteen, doing some sign painting at a local shopping center. It was a windy day, and I was using a very big and heavy extension ladder to reach the roof. There were a number of cars parked very close by. Dad happened to come along and he took the trouble to climb the ladder and say, "This wind could blow the ladder over when you're not standing on it. If it hits a car, it will cost a fortune. If I were you, I'd tie it down."

I decided that he wasn't me, and I didn't tie it down. About five minutes later, I was standing on the roof with my back to the ladder. I heard a big crash and turning around, looked down to see my ladder lying across the hood of a Toyota. The car was a mess and it cost me a fortune.

When I told Dad about it, he didn't say "You should have done what I told you," or "You're an idiot, kid." He just nodded. He knew that I had learned a lesson. He knew, as he always seemed to know, that sometimes it's best to say nothing.

IN A NUTSHELL

We don't always need to be talking. MANY TIMES, OTHERS APPRECIATE US MORE FOR WHAT WE DON'T SAY.

94

TAKING OFFENSE

Mature people don't get themselves upset over others' nasty remarks. From time to time, people say things to test us — comments like "you don't work too hard!" or "don't you eat a lot!" or "we all know you married him for his money!" Sometimes these things are said out of jealousy, but more often they're said to get a reaction. Whatever the motive, the best way to handle them is to smile and either say nothing or agree with the person!

So next time your neighbor sees you in your new car and says, "you don't do any work, yet they pay you a bunch!" you smile and say, "Isn't it great?" You don't have to explain about your responsibilities and your overtime. You don't need to justify yourself. Smile. Let it go.

When your sister-in-law moans, "You are always taking vacations!", you agree with her . . . "Yeah, we love vacations!" When Cousin Fred says, "Gee, you sure wasted some money on that swimming pool," you smile and say, "You bet! I hate cheap swimming pools!" Don't allow yourself to be upset. There is no gain in attacking Cousin Fred, or your sister-in-law, or the rest of them.

If you do any teaching or public speaking, you are bound to get hecklers who make personal remarks. Again, the best way to deal with rabble rousers is to agree with them in a good-natured way. When the fellow up in the back notes your spelling error on the blackboard and jibes, "You'd think our lecturer would know how to spell, wouldn't you?", you smile and say, "I agree! You'd think he would, wouldn't you?" If you start trying to defend yourself in front of a crowd, you are dead in the water! Either agree, or develop a selective hearing condition and stick to the subjects you want to talk about.

IN A NUTSHELL

Only little people make nasty remarks and only little people take offense. Be a big person.

AVOIDING ARGUMENTS

Never get in fights with pigs - you get all dirty and they enjoy it."
– General Abrams.

Have you ever spent an evening arguing with somebody, and felt you had wasted the whole evening? In fact, isn't that the way we often feel at the end of an argument?

Arguing is not good or bad – it's just arguing – but it can take up a lot of time and the more you try and change someone's mind, the less likely they are to change it!

WHY PEOPLE ARGUE

People tend to argue for three main reasons

1) They genuinely seek to change things. (These people are the REFORMERS.)

2) They want to be noticed. (The ATTENTION SEEKERS.)

3) They are feeling irritated and argumentative. (The FIGHTERS.)

If you are dealing with someone who seeks to change things through argument (a reformer), it will probably be appropriate to hear them out and

use the skills outlined in the last chapter. However, if you have an attention seeker or a fighter on your hands, it pays to recognize what is happening and decide not to play their game.

ATTENTION SEEKERS will argue purely for attention. They know that if they disagree violently with other people, they'll be noticed. (Fully functioning people choose love and affection rather than verbal conflict, but if our self-esteem is low, we will sometimes use arguments and tantrums to attract attention.

Teenage delinquents operate along this line of thinking. In trashing phone booths and wrecking the neighborhood, they employ a strategy which says, "You may not love me, but sooner or later, you won't be able to ignore me anymore!" Battered wives (and husbands) take the same approach, "You may not love me, but at least when you hit me, I'm getting noticed."

Other Attention Seekers take a less dramatic approach. You know the sort of person . . . You're having dinner with a party of six. Half-way through the main course of roast chicken, the woman opposite tells you it's not chicken but poached platypus. You know it's chicken. You cooked it! Why argue? Nod your head, smile and change the subject.

There will always be those who insist that "it's green" when it's yellow, "it's hot" when it's cold, "it's old" when it's new, "it's Bing Crosby" singing on the radio when you know it's Michael Jackson. Give yourself a break and let them believe what they want to believe. You don't have to educate them against their will. Allow them to do their thing and don't get involved.

FIGHTERS usually want to argue because they are irritated about something which has nothing to do with you. Again, you don't have to get involved. It is very simple to train the people in your life to be courteous toward you — just don't mess with them while they are kicking and screaming.

When your neighbor starts shouting obscenities over the phone, gently replace the receiver. If your house becomes a battle zone, with the rest of the family locked in arm-to-arm combat, take a walk in the park. You can return for the peace talks. There is no law which says, "If other people want to ruin their afternoon, you have to join them."

You teach people how to treat you by drawing a line . . . "I don't appreciate being shouted at. I will have nothing more to say to you until you stop throwing furniture across the living room." And then you leave.

WE DON'T HAVE TO AGREE

There are instances at home and at work when either everyone needs to agree or when people need to obey orders. At these times you may need to debate your viewpoint or lay down the law.

But there are countless instances when consensus is not important, when it matters not whether others agree with you – times when it is unimportant who is "right" and who is "wrong."

At these times life is simpler if we HAPPILY LET PEOPLE DISAGREE.

You may be thinking, "The theory of not arguing sounds fine, but how can you not argue if somebody vehemently disagrees with you?" YOU CHEERFULLY ALLOW OTHER PEOPLE TO HAVE A DIFFERENT POINT OF VIEW! YOU DECIDE NOT TO CARE TOO MUCH WHAT THEY THINK.

From infancy, we crave the support of those around us. We tend to operate on the formula, "Unless you agree with me, I'll shout, sulk, lose sleep, throw things and be very upset!"

Unless we review our personal philosophy in adulthood, we may still be operating with a similar program twenty-five years on – "Unless you agree with me (my football team, my religion, my politics, my beliefs), I'll shout, sulk, lose sleep, get drunk and be very upset – and I might even throw things!"

When others disagree with us, our insecurities surface. We tend to react. But if we rid ourselves of the addiction that everyone should see things our way, there is often no need to argue.

Let's imagine you have just sold your car for what I consider is an absurdly cheap price. I come along and say, "You're a fool for selling that car so cheaply!"

So you say, "What would you know?"

So I say, "More about cars than you!"

You say, "You're a know-it-all."

I say, "I know that you just lost yourself five thousand dollars!"

You say, "Why don't you mind your own *#*!* business!"

And I say, "You're a *@‼**!"

Quickly we fall into the argument trap, tempers flare and blood pressures rise. Now let's imagine that you allow me to have my opinion while you keep yours. The course of conversation may go like this . . .

"You're a fool for selling that car so cheaply!"

"You think I'm a fool?"

"Sure do."

"Well, if that's the truth for you, I respect that. I don't happen to agree, but I respect your right to your opinion."

In most cases, giving the other party room for their opinion will be enough to avoid argument. The moment we refuse to push our point of view, they stop pushing theirs.

Now one might say, "But if someone attacks you, and you feel that you are in the right, you can't just sit there and take it. Defend yourself!" Why defend yourself? You'll never please all of the people all of the time anyway. You can be doing better things with your time than trying to convince people against their will. Again, let them believe what they want.

IN A NUTSHELL

With attention seekers and fighters, scrap the notion which says, "If someone disagrees with me, my job is to change his mind." Try the philosophy, "If someone disagrees with me, my job is to let him do so." It makes life a lot easier.

TELLING PEOPLE "YOU 'RE WRONG!"

Be wiser than other people if you can;
but do not tell them so."
—Lord Chesterfield.

One of the surest ways to get attacked, berated, scorned, and abused by people is to tell them "YOU'RE WRONG." They just hate it – which usually means they'll hate you! Everyone wants to be right. When you tell them "YOU'RE WRONG", they generally add their own interpretation to your words. Often they read your meaning as "You're wrong, therefore there is something wrong with you." If it is important to have the other person appreciate your point of view or obey your instructions, look for any alternative.

"I respect your opinion – mine is a bit different ..."

"My experience doesn't match yours ..."

"I have a lot of respect for your opinion, but I don't agree with you on this one ..."

"I see that's the truth for you – the truth for me is ..."

Men fight duels, go to war, invest their fortunes, kill people to prove they are right! Being right is a serious business. If you want to reach an amicable agreement, speak of "opinions", "ideas", "different experiences" rather than "rights" and "wrongs".

ADMITTING YOU ARE WRONG

It is ironic. We seek others' respect by insisting we are RIGHT yet lose it. We fear losing others respect in admitting we are WRONG – yet often gain it.

Whenever we are prepared to admit we are wrong, people admire our courage and treat us with compassion – yet mostly we hate admitting to mistakes.

I don't have an outstanding record of admitting I am wrong either, but I am working on it. I am hoping that the writing of this chapter might encourage me to do more of it. What I have discovered is that when I am wrong, and I admit it, there is a great sense of relief. I have also found that the world doesn't end, nor do people ridicule me like they sometimes do when I insist I am right.

It stands to reason that if everybody wants to be right, and you are sometimes prepared to let others be right, you'll be appreciated for it.

IN A NUTSHELL

Telling people they are wrong is a great way to make enemies. Admitting you are wrong can be a good way to start a friendship.

HUMILIATING PEOPLE

When someone lets you down, you have a choice. You can criticize, humiliate and embarrass them or you can attempt to fix the problem.

Rarely can you do both. Some try for both. First they turn the other person into an enemy... "You are thoughtless, late, useless, ignorant..." Then they ask for support... "and now that I have abused you, give me my money back, fix my car, love me like you used to!"

BILL, YOU'RE WRONG *AND STUPID!*

It is a tough way to get results! No matter how upset we are, we need to remember that attacking others sabotages our chances of having them help us out.

If you like to confront people and have the occasional showdown, fine. But rarely does it help you get what you want. When you start out attacking people, they simply assume that you're rude. Suddenly they want to see you suffer, and if you are depending on them for cooperation, they'll see to it that you do suffer.

Imagine that your car is parked on the street. You return to your vehicle to find that a Volkswagen is parked an inch behind your back bumper. There is a fence almost touching your front bumper. You have no room to move.

You find out that the owner of the Volkswagen is in a nearby office. If you march into the office and say, "I'm looking for the jerk who wedged me up against a fence!", how will you come out? He may move his car quite happily. He may also hide under his desk, tell you that he has lost his keys or prolong his telephone conversation by half an hour just to spite you. To get the best results from others, GIVE PEOPLE THE BENEFIT OF THE DOUBT.

Even when dealing with someone you believe is a crook, give them respect and tread carefully.

Let's imagine that you have bought a stereo system from a local store. You get it home and find the dealer has given you a cheaper amplifier than the one promised. You have a suspicion that he is crooked and that he intentionally cheated you.

If he has cheated you, and you accuse him of being a crook, then he has nothing to gain by giving you what you want. You have already "found him guilty", so he'll think, "If you call me a criminal, I'll be a criminal!" However, if you give him the benefit of the doubt, saying, "I know you'll

be embarrassed to find that you gave me the wrong unit," there is a chance he'll set things right. You look for the best in him so he will look for the best in himself.

(Also, if you accuse him of being a crook, and he has not intentionally cheated you, he won't be happy either. In either case, it pays to edit the personal abuse.)

Now, if you try the benefit of the doubt approach with no result, the next strategy may be to get tough! But when you get tough, leave out personal attacks. It is possible to take a tough line with someone, and still show them due respect.

IN A NUTSHELL

People are generally happy to match your expectations of them. When you respect them and treat them well, they will return that respect. If your objective is to get their cooperation, be generous with your respect. Most times, they will bend your way to help you out.

CRITICISM

Points to remember about criticism —

A) CRITICISM DOESN'T WORK
B) PEOPLE RARELY BLAME THEMSELVES
C) IF YOU BLAME OTHER PEOPLE, THEY BLAME YOU!

I t is OK for me occasionally to find fault with myself, but if you do it, that is a whole different matter!

It is fascinating, isn't it? It's OK for us to find little faults with our attitude, our mother, our face, our city, our friends, our figure, but if anyone else should find fault, look out!

Criticism is the fastest way to create resentment and destroy a relationship. Our egos are so fragile that strong disapproval hits us like a sledgehammer. The moment we are criticized, we justify, we blame, we shout. Often we leave.

We humans have a remarkable capacity to see ourselves as always the innocent party. Psychologists have noted that even the most vicious murderers and criminals do not believe that they are to blame for their actions. If you were to go down to the maximum security section of your local prison and interview the rapists and murderers, you'd soon discover that they are either "innocent" or "misunderstood", or both, and that someone else is to blame for their suffering. (Al Capone once lamented that he was branded a killer, a number one public enemy, yet all he had ever tried to do was help people!).

If murderers and crooks don't even hold themselves to blame, what would that suggest about people who cut you off on the freeway and customers who never pay their bills? THEY ALSO SAY IT'S NOT THEIR FAULT! Whatever it is, most people don't think it is their fault – another

reason why criticism doesn't work.

Criticism is destructive. If your secretary won't do the job, criticism will make her more lazy. If your son is wetting his bed, criticism will make him a chronic case. It paralyzes, angers and provokes. It is asking for trouble.

IF YOU MUST CRITICIZE...

PRAISE FIRST. If I say to you, "You're looking great. Your hair is immaculate, your shirt is beautiful and so are your trousers. Your socks match. The only place you might improve is with your shoes. Your shoes need to be polished," you probably wouldn't take much offense. You would feel that I am on your side.

Praise is the sugar which makes the medicine palatable. People are delicate creatures with short memories. You can tell your wife she is the

light of your life at breakfast, but when you criticize her sponge cake at lunchtime, be careful! If you want to see her bake another sponge cake so long as you both shall live, wax lyrical about the baked potatoes before you criticize the dessert.

In speaking of praise, I am advocating sincere praise, NOT FLATTERY. You can always find something to appreciate, so let the other person know it. Praise tends to be specific – "You handled that telephone call very well, and I liked the way you kept your cool," – while flattery is usually general in nature, "You're a great secretary." People can pick the difference.

ASSUME THAT YOU ARE REMINDING THEM. Our egos are such that we much prefer to be reminded than told. When you remind somebody, "John, I bet I'm telling you something you already know...", you are questioning their memory rather than their intelligence. Most people aren't embarrassed about having a less than perfect memory – but they hate to be told that they are foolish.

Therefore, you may find phrases handy like, "I've seen you do this well before. I think you may have temporarily forgotten..."

Or, "You have probably already thought of this idea...", can help you make your point.

ADMIT TO THE PROBLEM YOURSELF. The sting in criticism is usually the feeling that the other person is saying, "I'm better than you are."

If I say to you, "You are always late!", don't you immediately run through your memory banks to recall how many times I've been late for lunch, work, dinner , breakfast, movies, classes, and so on. Being late is not really the problem; it is the feeling that you're being put down.

When you admit to the problem, "One of my faults which I'm working on is my lateness. I notice that you are often running late too...", it is much easier to accept.

IN A NUTSHELL

If you want to preserve relationships and get results from people, you must be sensitive to their egos. Be honest and be encouraging. Where applicable –
1. PRAISE BEFORE CRITICIZING
2. "REMIND" RATHER THAN TELL PEOPLE
3. ADMIT TO THE FAULT YOURSELF
4. LOOK TO THE FUTURE RATHER THAN BLAME FOR THE PAST

ASK QUESTIONS FIRST

Andrea was fuming over the phone ... "You have billed me for that seminar when I already paid for it in full. I told you twice already that I owe you no money. You have upset me and you have upset my family! It's a disgraceful reflection on your business! I will be taking this further." She was a very angry lady.

As she slammed the receiver down, I said, "I will check it out and get back to you. Thank you for your call."

Five minutes later, a very embarrassed Andrea called me back ... "My husband has just found the check stub. I am so, so embarrassed. What can I say? I could have sworn I gave you more than the deposit. This is really terrible ..."

Andrea was not only kind enough to phone back and apologize, she sent us chocolates and flowers!

Veronica was given a toaster for Christmas. It quit toasting within a week. She was furious. She marched down to the local electrical store demanding service, action and a replacement toaster.

They looked at the unit, said they would be more than happy to oblige but for one detail – the toaster had been bought across the street.

The moral of these stories – get the information first. GET THE FACTS BEFORE OPENING YOUR BIG MOUTH. Before you start abusing the landlord, threatening the shopkeeper, fuming at the boss or barking at the employee, get ALL the facts.

Finding out first saves embarrassment or "foot in mouth disease". It also gives you knowledge and knowledge is power.

BEING OVERCHARGED

We all hate being overcharged, and some of us handle it better than others. Polly gets on the phone to her mechanic and says . . .

"You're ripping me off. You're nothing but a lowdown crook. I never asked you to replace the gearbox. I'll see you in court. I told you not to proceed with any work without consulting my husband."

The mechanic says, "I saw your husband this morning. I have his written authority right here!"

Polly makes a fool of herself and an enemy of her mechanic in less than a minute!

Again, the wise approach is to get the facts. Check out the other person's understanding, recall and viewpoint on the transaction. Be like a lawyer in court, gathering the evidence you may need later on.

"Do you remember what you quoted me?"

"Do you recall our conversation regarding price? What did you say?"

"Do you have a record of my payments to date?"

"Have you seen the bill that was sent to me? Do you believe it is correct?"

Often, a couple of intelligent questions will eliminate the problem.

Sometimes people forget promises. As soon as you clarify that they don't remember, you can say, "Well, I remember. It was three hundred dollars and here it is."

As you will have found, invoices and records can also be wrong. Questioning in a civil manner before we march into battle can sort it out and save a lot of embarrassment.

Similarly, when people don't arrive, don't deliver, or don't perform, questions are preferable to ultimatums . . . "Do you recall what I asked? . . what you promised? . . . whose responsibility this is?"

Another handy line of questioning is "WHAT IF?"

"If I could demonstrate that I have been overcharged what would you do?"

"If there has been a mistake on your part, will you drop the billing?"

Smart people play dumb and ask a lot of questions. You never learn anything when you talk. Get them talking and you listen.

FIND OUT –
a) WHAT THEY KNOW
b) WHAT THEY THINK
c) WHAT THEY'LL DO
before you open your mouth.
Other useful questions include . . .
"How do you see it ?"
"How would you feel if you were me?"
"If you were me, what would you do?"

IN A NUTSHELL

Any time you're negotiating with someone, and most people interactions are a form of negotiation, make it your policy to ASK QUESTIONS FIRST. You save embarrassment and you ensure that you speak from a position of power.

When you question people, you invite them to think along your lines – this is more tactful and successful than TELLING them how to THINK.

MAKING YOUR POINT WITH QUESTIONS ...

Nobody enjoys firing people (well, almost nobody!). When it is necessary to dismiss someone, or discipline someone, usually the best approach is with questions.

I have a friend, Charlie, who is a very skillful communicator. His secretary, Jenny, had a sour attitude and frequently argued with Charlie's wife, who also worked in Charlie's office. He decided to fire his secretary, and, in dismissing her, he wanted her to understand why she was losing her job and make the interview as painless as possible. He related the dialogue to me, and it is an excellent example of how the skillful use of questions enabled him to make his point.

"Jenny, how would you say your attitude has been while working here?"

"Not the best."

"We spoke about this before, didn't we?"

"Yes – my husband is giving me trouble at home."

"Should you be bringing that here?"

"I don't suppose so."

"Would you consider that you have argued a lot with my wife here at work?"

"I suppose."

"Do you see that problem improving?"

"I guess not."

"Tell me, given that my aim is to have a happy office and a happy marriage, who do you think would eventually have to go?"

"Errr ... me?"

"You see that you will have to go?"

"Yes."

"Then we agree."

"Yeah, I had better leave."

Jenny dismissed herself. Charlie didn't attack her or criticize her. Through the skillful use of questions, he made her see that she had to go.

This is an art. You can't just ask any old question, for example, "How would you like me to fire you?" You must have some idea of how the other person might answer your questions in order to make your point.

ANGER DOESN'T MOTIVATE

I t is perfectly OK to get frustrated or angry with people – an ability to express anger is healthy. But we shouldn't make the mistake of trying to motivate other people by getting angry and shouting at them.

Partners, friends, employees, and even our kids will sometimes ignore or willfully defy us until they sense that we are prepared to take action – "action" meaning all kinds of things – spanking, firing, leaving, disciplining, fining, withholding privileges and so on.

Here's what often happens – people ignore us until they know that we mean business. By the time we finally decide to ACT, we are shouting and screaming. When they respond to us, we get the idea that screaming works. It was really the action.

Example. Mother asks Willie to tidy his room. Willie knows that Mother isn't serious yet, and continues watching Batman.

Mother asks again. "Willie, please tidy your room." Willie knows from previous experience that Mother can be ignored for at least forty five minutes.

Mother speaks for the third time, "Willie, you tidy your room NOW."

Willie decides she's still only half serious, reckoning "I've got at least another three minutes of Batman."

"Willie, TIDY YOUR ROOM!"

"More threatening" thinks Willie, "but still not enough volume to be dangerous." Willie stays with the caped crusader. Mother is getting a head of steam. Willie studies mother. She's now red in the face but she's not shouting yet. He figures she's about two minutes away from exploding.

A minute elapses and Mother marches into the living room wielding a wooden spoon. She's shouting at the top of her voice and waving the spoon, YOU GET INTO YOUR ROOM THIS MINUTE OR I'LL SPANK YOU SO HARD ..."

Willie doesn't wait around for the full speech – she's got the spoon! Mother is taking ACTION. She's finally standing by her threats. Willie is now very scared and a little impressed.

Mother finally achieves the desired results and reasons, "It looks like I always have to scream to get any cooperation around here." But it wasn't the screaming, it was the SPOON.

Mother could have taken a different route. She could have looked William straight in the eye right at the beginning and said, "Willie, The time is now 4:15pm. You have until 5:30pm. to have your room tidied. I will not be speaking to you about this again. I will not be getting upset or raising my voice. If you tidy your room by 5:30 – according to the clock in the kitchen – I will appreciate it. If you don't, you won't be watching TV for a week. Do you understand? Are there any questions?"

If Mother is prepared to follow through with her stated conditions, Willie will soon learn. If Mother backslides, and lets him watch TV even when he doesn't tidy his room, she may soon need to revert to spoons and screaming.

People who get results follow through. They are prepared to act.

We obey policemen because they back up their promises with action. Policemen as a rule don't scream or cry a lot. They don't get down and thump the pavement, and shout and sob and wail and say, "I've told you seventeen times today and I'm now telling you for the very, very, very last time. Don't steal other people's things." Instead, their message is, "Steal something and we'll arrest you."

People who maintain respect and get results, maintain their self control. Prime ministers, presidents, admirals, judges, understand that shouting and screaming do not motivate people.

IN A NUTSHELL

Because we sometimes delay action until we reach screaming point, we may believe that it's the screaming that motivates people. It isn't. People take us seriously because of what we DO, not because of how loud we scream.

ESTABLISH THE RULES

IF LIFE IS A GAME, LET PEOPLE KNOW THE RULES!

Fred has a problem with his son, Johnnie. Fred regularly tells Johnnie to take out the garbage each week. Johnnie often doesn't do it. When Johnnie doesn't do it, poor Fred doesn't know how to handle it. He wonders, "Do I smack him, do I send him to his bedroom, do I cut out his allowance, do I try talking to him . . .?"

Julie has a similar problem with Karen, her secretary. Frequently she'll ask her to complete a stack of typing by the end of the day. They both know that it is a reasonable request, yet the typing never seems to get done in time. Again Julie's in trouble – and she can't smack Karen or send her to a bedroom. Julie wants to maintain happy relations in the office and is a little confused as to how best to handle things.

In situations like these. relationships can suffer. If others let us down, and we discipline them for letting us down, they get upset. Often they will see us as being nasty, unfair and unreasonable.

TELL THEM UP FRONT

The solution is usually to tell your children and your secretary ahead of time a) WHAT YOU WANT b) WHAT HAPPENS IF THEY DO IT c) WHAT HAPPENS IF THEY DON'T. This can be done in a very friendly way. Let's see how Fred might handle Johnnie . . .

Fred - "Johnnie, let's talk about you and the garbage."

Johnnie - "What?"

Fred - "Everyone has jobs to do around this house. Your job is to take out the garbage. Do you understand that?"

Johnnie - "Yes."

Fred - "I want you to take out the garbage EVERY week. Will you do that?"

Johnnie - "Yes."

Fred - "If you do it, our house will be nice and clean, you'll continue to get your allowance and I'll never give you any trouble over the garbage. Do you understand?"

Johnnie - "Yeah. Can I go now?"

Fred - "No. There's more. If you don't do your job, I want you to understand that you won't get your allowance that week. It won't mean that I don't love you or that I want to be mean. It is just the way things work around here. There are consequences if you do and consequences if you don't."

Johnnie - "OK"

Fred - "So tell me, Johnnie, what's the deal on the garbage?"

Johnnie - "I get paid so long as I take it out."

Fred - "And if you don't do it?"

Johnnie - "I don't get my allowance."

Fred - "Got it. Any questions on the agreement?"

Johnnie - "No."

Fred - "Good. I wanted you to know ahead of time so there'll be no confusion."

Now that Fred has established some rules, he has made his life a lot easier. So long as he doesn't back down under pressure, the garbage will be taken out and he'll have his son's respect. Should Johnnie decide not to take out the garbage, Fred can bank the money he is saving or pay the kid next door to take out his garbage.

Julie can take a similar approach with secretary Karen . . .

Julie - "I want these letters typed by the end of the day."

Karen - "OK"

Julie - "Will you finish these by 5:30?"

Karen - "Yes."

Julie - "It is important. If you do it, I'll be grateful."

Karen - "OK"

Julie - "Karen, I want you to understand ahead of time that these letters must be done before you leave. If they're not done by 5:30, you'll have to stay and finish them. Are you clear on that?"

Karen - "Yes."

If you watch a lot of parents and bosses operate, you'll see them getting themselves in all kinds of trouble. Either they don't lay down the rules or they're too weak to stick to the rules when the crunch comes.

For example, Mother takes the children to the beach. At 5:00pm she says, "Let's go home."

The kids say, "Wait a while!"

At 5:15pm she says "We're going home."

The kids say," Just a minute."

At 5:25 Mother says, "I really mean it this time!"

5:45pm comes and now Mother can't even find the children. Eventually they leave the beach at 6:30 and Mother is asking herself, "Why do these rotten kids do this to me?"

The truth is, Mother is doing it to herself! She is busily demonstrating to her kids that she doesn't really mean anything she says. She says, "I'm leaving!" but she doesn't leave. The kids know their mother is a wimp.

What should she do? At 4:50 she could tell her children, "We are leaving in ten minutes. If any of you are not in the car at 5:00pm, you'll be left behind." At 5:00pm she drives off, with or without the children. How long would it take the children to realize that mother means what she says? To make our life easy in the long term, we need to be serious and show some strength.

Watch parents with children in supermarkets! It is very educational.

Two year old Billie - "I want a chocolate."

Dad - "You can't have a chocolate."

Billie - "I want one."

Dad - "You can't have one."

Billie - "I want one."

Dad - "You can't have one."

Billie (screaming) - "I WANT ONE!"

Dad - "No!"

Billie, (beginning to kick and cry and bellow) - "I WANT ONE, I WANT ONE, I WANT A CHOCOLATE, I WANT A CHOCOLATE."

Dad - "Here's your chocolate."

Message from Dad - "If you scream and shout for long enough, I will give you what you want. Even when I say "No", I'll back down if you make enough noise. If you behave like a complete brat, you'll always get what you want."

Having given Billie another lesson in "How to get what you want by being obnoxious," Dad continues to wonder why his son gives him such a hard time!

What should Dad do? Simply tell Billie early in the proceedings, "Today you're not getting a chocolate. You can kick and scream, punch the wall, hold your breath — no chocolate. If you want to have a fit, OK, but no chocolate. Billie will get the message. Children are very fast learners.

GETTING COMMITMENT

There is a saying among business people which goes, "If you say something, it's nonsense — if the customer says it, it's fact." In this context, it means that PEOPLE AREN'T COMMITTED TO SOMETHING UNLESS IT COMES OUT OF THEIR OWN MOUTHS.

What does that mean? It means that it is no good just telling your daughter, "I want you to be home by eleven o'clock." Maybe daughter just thinks, "So YOU want me to be home by then!" Often daughter thinks, "I didn't hear that."

You need to go one step further. You need her answer on the subject. You look daughter in the face, eye to eye. You get her full attention, and you ask her, "Will you do it?" Get a commitment. This applies to any negotiation. Ask the person, "Are you going to buy it, finish it, arrive on time?" TELLING SOMEONE WHAT YOU WANT MEANS NOTHING UNLESS YOU KNOW THAT a) THEY HEARD YOU b) THEY UNDERSTAND YOU and c) THEY'RE COMMITTED.

Sometimes we're scared to ask for their commitment because we fear they'll say "No". That's being weak.

IN A NUTSHELL

People get away with what they know they can get away with. To make your life easier, and get results with others –

a) TELL THEM FIRST, "This is what I want. These are the consequences."

b) Check that they understand.

c) Find out what they are prepared to do. GET THEIR RESPONSE.

d) Having committed yourself to a course of action, follow through.

LEARN FROM YOUR MISTAKES

Harry arrives home late from work. His wife slams the meal on the table, shouting, "Where do you think you've been? YOU'RE LATE!" He has been arriving late for twenty-eight years. She's been angry with him for twenty-eight years. She shouts, he sulks.

Question. After a quarter of a century together, shouldn't they have learned something about human relations? Shouldn't she have figured out a better way to encourage her husband to arrive home on time?

What if she had said, "Darling I'm so glad you are home. Whenever you are late, I miss you so much!" Would that get a different reaction?

As the years go by, shouldn't we get better at being happy? Shouldn't we, with practice, refine our abilities to get along with family members and join that joyous minority of people who just get happier with every passing year?

I had a neighbor who was prone to breaking things over her husband's head. She would rip cupboard doors off of their hinges and smash them over his skull! If you were to drop by on a Sunday morning, you would likely see one of her weapons leaning against the fridge – with a head size hole in it. As her spouse ate his cornflakes, she would point to the

hole and he would show you his flat head! She also enjoyed throwing glasses of milk over him at parties.

Because these two had been married for around twenty-four years, it occurred to me that somewhere along the line they ceased learning about communication and human relations.

Some things just don't work! Breaking furniture over your partner is one, but there are other more subtle things which undermine relationships.

When we greet our partner with –

"Where have you been?"

"What do you think you're doing?"

"You're ALWAYS late!"

"It's your fault."

"You're dumb, fat, lazy, ignorant, selfish and hopeless."

The effect is bad. We need to learn from experience and not continue to make the same old mistakes.

For example, when someone is repeatedly late, our message needs to be, "I enjoy your company so much that when you're late, I miss you. I feel that you don't care and that makes me upset . . ." We need to be giving them incentive to comply with our wishes, not incentive to leave home. What usually happens is that the "offended" party begins to nag and the late arrival begins to arrive later and later to avoid the nagging.

One fellow, Robert, whose wife was quite unfriendly whenever he arrived home late, phoned her from the office one evening to warn her that he would not be home in time for dinner. He asked her to put his meal in the oven and to his surprise she was very obliging. Only when he arrived home did he discover why she was so delighted to pop his meal in the oven – dinner that night was salad!

We're talking about very elementary communication skills here – and about things we all know – but it helps to be reminded about the basics sometimes.

IN A NUTSHELL

We should expect constant improvement in our relationships rather than gradual deterioration. A relationship is like a business – it's either getting better or it's getting worse – there's no standing still. IF THINGS AREN'T IMPROVING, THEN WE ARE LIVING WITHOUT LEARNING.

YOU GET WHAT YOU EXPECT

In the late 1960's, Dr. Robert Rosenthal of Harvard University ran an experiment in a school in California. The school principal called three teachers into his office at the beginning of the year and told them, "Based on your teaching excellence over the last three or four years, it's clear that you are the best teachers in the school. As a reward, you will each be given a class of 30 of the brightest students in the school to teach for this year. The students' selection would be based on their high IQ's and on their keenness to do well." He added, "Teach the children as you would teach any other class, and do not tell them or their parents that you know they are special."

At the end of the year, these three classes led the entire school district in academic accomplishment, performing at twenty to thirty percent above average.

The principal then dropped his bombshell on the teachers . . . "These students were not chosen for their academic ability — they were chosen out of a hat." Surprised, the three teachers could only reason that the students had excelled because they, the teachers were brilliant. Bombshell number two . . . the teachers had also been chosen out of a hat!

The teachers BELIEVED in themselves and they EXPECTED that the children would do very well, and the children proved them correct.

The message for us: people, that is, your son, your brother, your secretary, the kids you coach at football, even your spouse, will tend to perform according to your expectations. If you think you're managing an indifferent team, they'll lose and prove you right. When you believe in people, they believe in themselves, and again they tend to prove you right.

You say, "But everyone knows that! There's not a book on parenting or personnel management that doesn't talk about the importance of praise and encouragement." Right! There's lots of talk about it but few people KNOW it. When people really KNOW something, they use it in their life. Ask yourself how many teachers or bosses you've had who have encouraged and inspired you to exciting new heights.

WHAT DO I EXPECT FROM PEOPLE?

Rosenthal's findings should give us all cause to consider, "What have I been expecting from the people in my life?" Fred says, "Well that's OK for

Rosenthal but I KNOW that my secretary is a dope!" That's just it, Fred. While you "know" she's a dope, she'll stay dopey. When you start to believe in her, and encourage her, and support her, she may start to show new promise.

We can all be a bit like Fred, expecting to be disappointed and having our expectations realized.

SO, HOW DO I ENCOURAGE PEOPLE?

You get people to expect success by helping them to see their progress. Often it's hard for them to see it for themselves. You take your new recruit to one side and you say, "Jim, in the space of a week, you're really getting a feel for this job. It's early days yet, but with your skills and personality, I can see you running this department in a year or two."

You begin to paint pictures in Jim's mind of greater possibilities. You get him to see himself as a success. Getting people to expect of themselves is not just a matter of praising them, although it involves praise. It also involves taking them into the future. You say, "Son, I know that you've had a tough time with mathematics. But just imagine if you were to spend an extra half hour a night on these equations. With your determination, I could see you getting straight A's by next term. How would that feel?"

IN A NUTSHELL

You can't make others do things they don't want to do, but nearly everyone wants to feel successful and appreciated. Recognize people's worth and potential. PRAISE THEM SPECIFICALLY and tell them WHAT THEY CAN ACHIEVE and WHY YOU BELIEVE IT. They'll respond.

FORM WINS FRIENDS

Most of us have weathered endless lectures from families and teachers on the importance of manners. "Be courteous. Say thank you. Brush your hair. Take your feet off the table. Don't talk with your mouth full. DON'T shovel your peas like that! That's a knife, not a pencil. And next time, use your handkerchief!"

We might have wondered why it was so important that we prove that "mother brought us up properly" or that we understood what manners were all about.

Of course, good manners are not about proving anything. Manners are designed to enable others to feel comfortable in our company. Manners amount to an awareness of ourselves out of respect for other people.

To affect others positively, you don't have to wear the latest designer jeans. You don't need to serve champagne in Swedish crystal. A successful evening doesn't hinge on whether you serve your soup from the right or the left.

Manners are but a part of the person – in a sense, a facade, but still important. Should we exaggerate their importance, though, we risk over-looking people's good points . . . he eats like a horse (but he's generous to a fault), she wore a T shirt to the formal dinner (but she told great stories), their glasses don't match (but their house is full of laughter).

In our bid to be courteous, let's not become obsessed by surface issues.

Isn't it frustrating when you ask your friend to tell you about her boss, and she says, "Well, he's tall, brown hair, he wears a Rolex watch, he has a nice house, knows his food, he looks a bit like . . ."? Get to the real issues. Is he funny? Does he talk about his sculpture? How does he spend his time? Is he a kind man?

WHAT IS FORM?

Form is another word for style. And here the understatement is often better. Let's take an example.

Agnes marries the only son of the affluent Schafers and on the death of Grandmother Schafer, inherits a vault of gems. Suddenly Agnes, of middle class background, surrounded by middle class family and friends, is worth an absolute mint – and has the jewelry to prove it. It might be a temptation to flaunt her newly acquired riches.

But Agnes is aware of good form and displays remarkable style. When there's a gathering of the Schafer clan, and all the relatives arrive bedecked in old diamonds, Agnes wears an elegant outfit with nothing but a string of pearls and matching earrings. Everyone expects her to arrive looking like a pawn shop, but she doesn't. She chooses not to compete. Result? Agnes wins respect.

Good form is choosing to understate rather than overstate. It's not competing. It's knowing you don't have to prove anything.

DRESSING UP

If you wish to make friends (or keep them), be courteous in planning what to wear.

Rule One: DON'T OVERDRESS. People resent it.

Rule Two: BE NEAT. Half the battle is won if you are neat. It doesn't matter if your lapel is outdated. At least you can be tidy. People expect and appreciate neatness. If you can't pay your rent, at least you can brush your hair and clean your shoes. People notice the little things.

Rule Three: HAVE A SENSE OF OCCASION. People appreciate it. Look at the invitation and observe the dress code. If it is not stated, ask. While it's inappropriate to wear jeans to a wedding reception (unless it's specified "wear Levi's"), neither is it correct to wear a Scarlet O'Hara taffeta gown which might totally eclipse the bride; or a suit five times more expensive than the groom's.

KNOW WHEN TO LEAVE CENTER STAGE

Good form is also about knowing when to take a back seat . . .

Rod Fuller's company is taken over and Rod receives a month's notice. Being a father of four with a mortgage, it is a heavy blow to Rod's financial position and his career ambitions. Rod feels shattered.

Ironically, Rod's brother, Don, gets a substantial promotion that same week. At a birthday party attended by Rod and Don, their families, and half the neighborhood, friends are commiserating with Rod and offering words of encouragement. In the midst of the conversation, Don's wife calls to the group, "Let's drink to Don's promotion. Today he was appointed general manager." A person with a better self-concept and more consideration would have chosen a different time for the announcement.

IN A NUTSHELL

There is no disputing that good presentation and eating with your mouth shut will make your life more pleasant. (I know of at least one financial wizard who has been excluded from the board of a huge organization simply because the board members say he's a pig.)

But manners are not so much about knowing every last principle of table etiquette. When defining manners, think less in terms of unbreakable rules and more in terms of CONSIDERATION, RESPECT and MAKING PEOPLE COMFORTABLE.

On the whole, aim for STYLE and GOOD FORM. Consider others' feelings and you'll be appreciated.

EXPECTATIONS IN A FRIENDSHIP

Reflecting on past relationships, people often talk of disappointments..."I was her best friend until she went and did THAT"..."He let me down"..."She never treated me as an equal..."

If we know what we expect of a friendship, and if our expectations are REASONABLE, then it's less likely that we'll be disappointed.

I had a friend, James. James was one of the most unreliable and terminally running late people I ever met. For a long time I let this irritate me. Eventually it dawned on me that James was James – enormously likeable and equally irresponsible.

It was not for me to change his ways. I had to adjust MY EXPECTATIONS of the friendship. I had to be more accepting. He was simply a fun person to be around – a great conversationalist, witty, generous, and interested in everything from motor bikes and aquariums, to photography and laying bricks. If and when he ever arrived, his company was a bonus. When I changed my expectations about his behavior, we had a lot more good times and less arguments. (Last I heard, he was living on a tropical island where everyone else runs as late as he does.)

Look at a father-son relationship. Son says, "Dad always treats me like a little boy. Why can't he see me as an adult?"

Because, to your Dad, you're always a little boy. There's no way around it. Fathers are always older than their sons! That's the deal in having a Dad – you get a guy who thinks you're a kid when you're fifty! And sons have dealt with that one since Adam. Once you accept it – once you adjust your expectations – it's not such a problem.

Every friendship is different. You can't expect to have the same relationship with your boss that you have with your fellow employees. You probably won't relate to your accountant like you relate to your doctor. People have different, values, experiences, positions, and these factors affect friendships.

Also remember that what we want out of a friendship may not be what our friend wants. Observe closely. People are always dropping broad hints centered on their wants and needs. If they sound vague, make them elaborate. The conversation will be rewarding.

LIMITS OF FRIENDSHIP

Y ou can be honest with friends. You can depend on friends. Friends you can open up to. All true. But there are also limits to any friendship.

What kind of limits? Limits like –

• USING FRIENDS

Barry may be your buddy, but don't figure that you can borrow money from buddy Barry every other day of the week. Eventually Barry will decide he's being used as a bank and he'll foreclose on the friendship.

The neighbors will be thrilled to babysit your twins a couple of times a year. They may happily do it every few months. They might even agree to do it every month. But press the favour to once a week and suddenly those friendly neighbors of yours will quit answering the telephone. Meanwhile, you're saying, "What's happened to the Parkers? We were such good friends!"

People love to help, but they hate being used. Friendship and support is a two-way street. You need to monitor the traffic.

• ABUSING FRIENDS

BEING CLOSE TO PEOPLE IS NO EXCUSE TO INSULT THEM.

Gloria says, "If I can't insult my best friend, who can?" Well Gloria, just because she's your friend doesn't mean she hasn't got feelings. Bill says, "Of course I poke fun at her big nose. She's my wife." WRONG!

We each have delicate egos. Friendship calls for sensitivity and tact. Familiarity is fine and wonderful. But let's beware of offending. I may be your friend, but if I repeatedly joke about your looks and question your intelligence, you'll soon look elsewhere for company. No matter how close a friendship, there's always room for tact.

LOOKING TO OTHERS

Your challenge in life is to be true to yourself.

HUGS

Hugging is healthy! We need to be touched – and often. But sometimes we fear rejection, so we resort to patting babies and dogs. We're at least confident that the neighbor's poodle won't turn and say, "Hands off me, you jerk!"

Now even the medical experts are saying WE NEED TO HUG EACH OTHER, not just the dog. Senior Psychiatrist at the Menninger Foundation, Dr. Harold Falk, says "Hugging can lift depression, enabling the body's immunization system to become tuned up. Hugging breathes fresh life into tired bodies and makes you feel younger and more vibrant."

Dr. Bresler at the U.C.L.A. pain clinic gives hug prescriptions – "get your hug in the morning, a hug at lunchtime, one at dinner, one before bed and you'll feel better."

In her book, "The Joy of Touching", Helen Colton explains that the hemoglobin in the blood increases significantly when you are touched and hugged. Because it's the hemoglobin that carries the vital supplies of oxygen to the brain, heart and throughout the body, hugging begins to look very important.

Of course, people may say, "I'm not the hugging kind." But it is still possible to become the hugging kind. You don't have to hug everyone, but you have to get your share of hugs from somewhere.

It also seems that as we become less self-conscious, we warm to the idea of being hugged. The tendency is always that people grow to like being hugged and to depend on them rather than the reverse. You don't meet too many people who say, "I used to hug a lot and I hated it. I gave it up. I'm glad no one hugs me anymore."

JUDGING PEOPLE

When people talk about an ideal friendship, they nearly always mention "acceptance" and "non-judgment"... "he never judges me...", "she accepts me as I am...", "he loves me regardless..." They're saying, "I can get close to people when they don't judge and criticize me."

In effect they're saying that whenever we cease to judge and analyze people, we get closer to them. The reverse is also true. When we analyze and criticize others, we create distance.

Now Fred may say, "But I'm intelligent. I'm an intellectual. I have to make judgments about people all the time." Maybe so, Fred, but at some point it pays to draw the line. Take a page from the Taoists' book. You don't have to judge everybody – it's possible to appreciate people just for their uniqueness – like you might enjoy a rose or a song. You don't always have to analyze them, criticize them and pick them apart.

NON-JUDGMENT AND PEACE OF MIND

When we cease constantly to judge others, we find greater peace of mind. How often do we hear people criticizing how their friends live?

"She's far too fat to wear that frilly dress!"

"He's a fool to marry that woman!"

"Frank should get off his behind and get a proper job!"

"They should know better than to spend all that money on a BMW!"

Familiar? When we judge what others should be doing with their time, their money or their life, we sabotage our own peace of mind – we allow ourselves to be disturbed that things are not as they "should be." Greater happiness comes from accepting others as they are. When we set out to change people, we get stressed and they hate us for it!

There will always be loafers, crooks, boasters, workaholics, alcoholics, spendthrifts, transvestites, rich people, poor people, fat people, thin people, and lots more kinds of people on the planet, regardless of what you think about it. If you are flexible and let others be, you save yourself a lot of unnecessary stress. PEACE OF MIND COMES FROM A CHANGE OF ATTITUDE, NOT CIRCUMSTANCES. And who are we to judge what other people should be doing?

Also, because we learn so much from our mistakes, isn't it sensible to let others create their "mistakes" and learning experiences, while we concentrate on improving our own lives?

HAVING OPINIONS

Many of us grow up believing that intelligent people should have an opinion about absolutely everything. "This is good, this is bad, that is outrageous." Newspapers express opinions, politicians have opinions, current affairs shows have opinions, next door neighbors have opinions – "be concerned about this" and "be outraged about that".

You don't always have to have an opinion. Sometimes it is appropriate to have no opinion at all. Why not just let people be? When your neighbor says, "Don't you think Frank should get a job?" you may like to say, "I think Frank should do what he wants." When she says, "Isn't it terrible that Frank's wife is so overweight?" you say to yourself, "Perhaps she's learning about being fat."

Sometimes, of course, it's necessary to pass opinions or make an assessment of people, for example, "Does my secretary produce results?", "Is my accountant doing his job?" But there are many times when it's unproductive to pass judgment.

Try this experiment. Spend a week not judging anything or anybody. When next you meet someone who talks a lot, or spends a lot or complains a lot or doesn't work, mentally say to yourself, "I give you the space to experience life as you choose. It is not for me to judge you." Life becomes a lot more serene.

A "non-judgmental" attitude does not mean that you have to "like" everybody, or that you don't have preferences – it means that you adopt an attitude where you are more at peace with those around you.

There will be times when you choose not to be in another's company, but this can stem more from an attitude of what feels right for you rather than from condemnation of other people's differences.

IN A NUTSHELL

If Fred has spent the past forty five years being irritated by others, it may dawn on him that lots of people don't see things his way. If he wants to be happier, he then has two options – either wait for everyone to start thinking like him or grant them the right to live their lives the best way they know how.

GOSSIP

There's a fascinating game you can play which demonstrates how drastically information gets distorted in the process of being passed from one person to another.

Twenty or so people stand in a circle. One person whispers a message in the ear of the person on his left. The receiver of the message in turn whispers the message to the person on his left, and so the message is passed around the circle. This would seem to be a simple exercise, except that when the message finally gets back to the person who sent it, it's always a totally different message. "John Brown lost his wallet in the neighborhood" becomes "Jan Smith is pregnant." In the space of three minutes you see the birth of a juicy rumor.

You may like to remember this exercise when someone repeats a little gem of information they've just heard. From time to time, someone will be bursting to tell you, "James thinks you're crazy for doing this!", "Jenny never wants to see you again," "William says you're a hopeless idiot . . ." Be skeptical about such gossip.

Something else to remember about secondhand news – if you don't hear it first-hand, you don't know HOW it was said. Is it important to know HOW something is said? Read the following sentence and watch the meaning change when the emphasis is put on a different word –

I didn't say she stole my money.

I didn't say she stole my money. (but SOMEONE said it).
I **DIDN'T** say she stole my money. (I DEFINITELY didn't say it).
I didn't **SAY** she stole my money. (but I INFERRED it).
I didn't say **SHE** stole my money. (but SOMEONE stole it).
I didn't say she **STOLE** my money. (but she did SOMETHING with it).
I didn't say she stole **MY** money. (she stole SOMEONE ELSE'S).
I didn't say she stole my **MONEY**. (she took SOMETHING ELSE).

Eight different meanings without changing one syllable! Tone, inflection and emphasis are everything in conversation. Unless you hear the words said, you can't possibly assess accurately what is meant by a given comment.

Before you believe ANYTHING, before you have a heart attack, fire your manager or file for divorce, go to the source and get the information firsthand. This is basic advice, but we can all get caught if we're not careful.

IN A NUTSHELL

Though gossip may start out based on fact, the facts soon evaporate. Where possible, get the real story from the horse's mouth before you act.

If you believed everything you heard about everyone you met, you might trust very few people and have few friends. Obviously, if the whole town swears that Honest Harry is a two-timing gangster, you may want to take heed, but for the most part, take people as you find them and don't be swayed by rumor. Make up your own mind.

GIVING

Mary gives Fred a $500 present for his birthday. When Mary's birthday comes, Fred arrives with a bunch of daisies. Mary is stunned. She mutters, "What a cheapskate! I spent a week's paycheck on your birthday, and you give me pathetic flowers!"

Conventional attitudes might suggest that Fred has let Mary down, that there hasn't been a fair exchange. But giving is not a matter of EXCHANGING. When you give, you GIVE.

You give someone a present because you want him to have it. You give it because you want to give it. If you don't want to give anything, that's perfectly OK, too.

Where we get into trouble is when we "give" with strings attached. Mary's message on the card reads "Happy Birthday, Fred. I hope you like the stereo. All my love, Mary." The unwritten message is "My birthday is in August, Fred. If you don't spend at least as much on me, you're a cheap jerk and you can go find another girlfriend."

Problems arise when we give with conditions – "I want you to have this sweater. If you don't wear it twice a week, I'll be very offended." Trying to control people is always a frustrating business. If you give me a sweater, it should be because you're happy for me to do with it as I see fit. You'll stay much happier if you respect my decisions on what I do with it once it's mine.

Similarly, we may give to others in the form of sacrifice, giving up our time or our opportunities in favor of spouses, our children or our friends. Then we tell them, "I sacrificed for you!" to make sure they know about it so they can feel bad. "I gave up the best years of my life – I sacrificed my career."

Be adult about it. Make your choice. If you want to do it, do it. If you don't, don't. Leave out the sacrifice talk. Let the person be grateful – don't make him feel guilty.

As far as giving and receiving go, we basically get back what we give out in this world. Sometimes we receive from unexpected sources and don't receive from the "expected" ones. The only way to maintain peace of mind as a giver is to give without conditions. If Mary can give Fiancee Fred his stereo with the thought "I'm so happy to give you this stereo, so you may do with it as you please," she'll stay happy whatever Fred does – whether he listens to it daily, whether he gives it to his brother, whether Fred runs off and marries someone else.

When we're making a gift, we should aim to give without strings.
If we say, "Take this . . .
a) provided you appreciate IT
b) provided you appreciate ME
c) provided you do with it what I want you to do with it
d) provided I GET SOMETHING in return
e) provided you feel guilty. . .
then we're not giving at all. We're EXCHANGING.

Giving without conditions may sound like "spiritual advice". It is also very practical, and it can eliminate a lot of resentment.

JEALOUSY

Freud said that those who claim they are never jealous are deluding themselves. Most of us feel a little jealous from time to time — someone we care about gives their attention to our best friend, a colleague gets a promotion, and it hurts a little.

We may tend to believe that there is only so much love and affection to go round. Then, if mother shows some extra affection to our sister, we feel less worthy. We don't have to live like that.

If your mother adores your sister, it doesn't make you less wonderful. If your wife thinks your brother is cute or intelligent or entertaining, it doesn't mean she loves you less. There is plenty of room for lots of special people in the world.

MAKING OTHERS HAPPY

It is not your responsibility to MAKE others happy. Your challenge in life is to be true to yourself, to experience as much as you can, to treat others as you like to be treated, and above all, to ENJOY your life. Your job is not to FORCE people around you to be happy.

If your neighbor wants to be miserable, frustrated and gloomy, it is his perfect right to be so. Misery is a stage in the learning process of life. If a person chooses to be permanently depressed, let him be so.

Think back on your own life. You may remember times when you were depressed, and friends said to you, "Snap out of it! Life is great!" But you weren't ready to decide life was great, were you? Only when YOU were ready did you change your attitude and begin to see things differently.

Anyway, who are we to tell others they HAVE to be happy? If God doesn't descend from the clouds and force happiness upon the gloomy, who are we to decide how they should behave?

Consider for a moment your greatest mistakes. They may have been marriages, divorces, failed business ventures, jobs that didn't work out, lost friendships and so on. Now stop reading for a moment and review what you learned from those mistakes. STOP READING!

OK, what did you learn? Didn't you learn a lot? We learn so much from our mistakes — success we celebrate, failure we contemplate. So whenever you march in to "save" somebody from a silly marriage, trip, move, divorce, you are very possibly robbing them of a major learning experience. Can you justify doing that?

FOR YOUR OWN PEACE OF MIND...

You can go crazy trying to change people — and meanwhile, they'll hate you for it. Let's say you have a neighbor, Dreary. Dreary moans about the government, the economy, his mother, he complains about the weather and the price of groceries, he tells you that people are horrible and the world is going downhill, he worries about his health ... everything is a problem and nothing is worth the effort.

Dreary is miserable and a pain in the backside because he has chosen to be that way. No one is holding a gun to his head and saying, "Dreary, you have to be a pain in the backside." He is acting out of choice. He looks at his options, and decides that TO BE HAPPY WOULD BE TOO DIFFICULT AND TAKE TOO MUCH EFFORT. He decides it's easier to be miserable and drag others down at the same time.

Just as Dreary acts out of choice, you can do the same thing — choose to let him be dreary by himself. You say, "What if Dreary is an old friend?" Choose some new friends!

If you have miserable people around you who drag you down and sap your energy, and they refuse to change, change company. Don't hate them, don't resent them or judge them. Love yourself and others enough to leave them alone and mind your own business. When you leave, don't make a performance of it, don't announce that you are better than they are, just spend your time elsewhere.

WHAT IF PEOPLE COME FOR HELP?

Helping people when they have asked for help is a whole different matter to judging how others should live, and then setting out to change them. Helping those who are committed to progress is a joyous experience.

If you have found a way to make your life work, and someone says, "You are always happy – how do you do it?", share your ideas, give them your time, lend them your books. But marching out into the world and telling others to reform is a frustrating business and they'll resent you for it.

I once attended a seminar with William, a friend of mine. At the seminar we met Leo, a self-confessed compulsive worrier. He didn't know how to enjoy himself and could never spoil himself. He was working eighty hours a week and his family life was full of tension. He drank himself to sleep each night.

The three of us spent some time together during the week, and I noticed that Leo asked us questions here and there about our approach to life. The seminar ended and I lost contact with Leo.

Six months later, Leo was in town and he rang me, insisting that he must buy me dinner. He said,

"Andrew, I owe you dinner!"

"How come?"

"You'd be amazed to know what's happened since I saw you. I have cut back my working hours. I'm spending more time with my family, the business is sailing along and I haven't drunk myself to sleep in six months, I've bought a nice car ..."

I said, "That's fantastic! Why do you owe me dinner?"

"Because meeting you two guys made a difference for me."

"Really? How is that?"

"Spending a week with you two, I saw that you were happier and more relaxed than I was. You inspired me to make some changes. I want to thank you."

I said, "Thank you, Leo, but you deserve the credit – you did it. But you can still buy me dinner."

It was a joy to receive Leo's call. I was happy to know that his life was going well and to feel that I had made some contribution. His call also reinforced my belief that when somebody is really ready to change something in his life, he'll do it. We can avoid much frustration and ill feeling by not lecturing them before they're ready. People don't need you to shove your ideas down their throats.

IN A NUTSHELL

When others are really enthusiastic, they come and ask for the information. PEOPLE MUST BE READY FOR CHANGE. You don't have to spread your gospel just in case. If you are bursting to help people, you don't need to preach. Just BE AN EXAMPLE. People will be drawn to you and will ask your advice. If no one is asking you, play golf.

WHEN SPENDING TIME WITH MISERABLE PEOPLE...

I was once a guest on a radio talk show, answering questions about my book "Being Happy!" A woman phoned the station and said, "Mr. Matthews, you should be ashamed of yourself — that you should talk of being happy when other people in the world are in pain and misery — I think it's selfish and disgraceful!"

Her reaction was a little extreme, but she raised a valid point. How do we reconcile our own happiness with the misery of those around us? What if, in the short term, it's difficult to avoid the presence of morose individuals? How do you deal with them? Is it OK to be joyous if your coworkers are suicidal?

If you really care about your melancholic fellow employees, wouldn't you get down and be miserable with them? NO! Be happy for your own sake and let them make their own choices. Love people enough to let them make their own decisions.

If you are surrounded by miserable people, and it is difficult to avoid their company, the best thing you can do is be happy! If you wallow in another's misery, then you're both miserable. That helps no one, and you become a victim.

When others are unhappy, have compassion, but at the same time serve yourself by keeping your own spirits high. You then demonstrate joy and laughter as an alternative. Many people use depression as an attention seeker. If you choose to join them in their depression, you allow yourself to be manipulated. Refuse to play their game, and they'll often quit, and you'll both be better off.

WHEN PEOPLE ARE HAPPIER THAN YOU!

We also need to be able to deal with other people being happier than we are. If our partner is having a wonderful time, we can sometimes be thinking to ourselves, "She seems to be deliriously happy and I'm left out," or worse, "His happiness doesn't seem to have anything to do with anything I've done or said. How dare he be happy without me!"

Insisting that we should get the credit for the happiness of the ones we love leads to jealousy and discontent. Happy people are happy to see others happy. They free themselves of the attitude, "I want you to be happy SO LONG AS IT'S WITH ME!"

MORE THOUGHTS ON TRYING TO CHANGE PEOPLE

"GOOD PEOPLE ARE FOUND, NOT CHANGED!"
– Jim Rohn.

In his business seminars, Jim Rohn tells the story of how he began his own business. He would take undermotivated, under-enthused, unreliable people, hire them, and then try and make them motivated, reliable and enthusiastic. He found it a tough assignment. Says Rohn, "I decided I would change them even if it killed me – I ALMOST DIED!" Rohn learned quickly that the sensible approach was to find people who shared his values, and hire THEM.

If you're hiring people, you can save yourself years of distress by applying this principle. You build a happy, enthusiastic team by hiring happy, enthusiastic people. People are the way they are because that's the way they are. Changing either hasn't occurred to them or isn't attractive to them and probably seems like too much work anyway. Apart from the fact that it is an infringement on another person to force them to change, it rarely works. If you need a neat secretary, don't choose a slob and try to change her. Don't choose someone who is unreliable and expect to make them responsible. Don't hire a bunch of liars and try to make them honest.

The same goes for husbands and wives. If you like your men sober, don't marry a drunk! This is basic advice, but it often happens where one partner sets out to "control" the other. For example, the wife decides to control her husband. He resents it. She hates him for not loving her enough to change. He hates her for not loving him as he is. Result: everyone is unhappy.

IN A NUTSHELL

In choosing people to live with or work with, find people whose values approximate your own. Ask yourself the question, "If he changed nothing about himself, would I be happy to live (or work) with this character?" If the answer is "NO!", keep looking.

WHO'S PERFECT?

"My friend is not perfect − nor am I − and so we suit each other admirably."
− Alexander Pope

The more that we accept others as they are, and not demand that they be perfect (or be like us), the happier our relationships become. Also, if we can understand a little of why others behave as they do, we will be more tolerant. For example ...

I have a friend, Jenny. Jenny has a problem with money − not that she doesn't have it − she's got mountains of it, but she can't bear to part with it. If five of you go out to dinner and the bill comes to $151.35, she'll get out her calculator, which she always takes to restaurants, and give you the breakdown... "OK That would be $30.27 each BUT I didn't have garlic bread so I owe $30.27 less four times 15 cents minus, the five cents which you borrowed from me last Thursday week ..." She is almost unbelievable!

She is also a very fine, honest, caring person. I like to look at her good points and understand that perhaps somewhere in her past she had a mother or a husband or some experience which helped shape her attitude toward money. I figure that it is far better to give her space to behave as she sees fit rather than to get indigestion over her financial approach. She has so many qualities. If I were to dismiss her because of her money quirks, I would lose a fine friend.

Ralph is another pal. Ralph is wonderful company − humorous, interested, well-informed, happy, enthusiastic, intelligent, successful − all of which he'll happily admit to. You see, Ralph is not the most modest fellow in the world and he loves to talk about himself. But I value his company enormously.

From one point of view it would be possible to say, "Ralph is a know-it-all!" and write him off. But that would be a shame because he has so much to contribute. I've learnt so much from him and had so many laughs with him. If Ralph was to be more like other people, he wouldn't be Ralph!

You don't need to be a psychologist to make allowances for people, or to appreciate what kinds of experiences might have shaped their attitudes. All you need is a commitment to make your life richer.

If we set aside our prejudices and instead have preferences, it becomes a lot easier to appreciate others. If a person eats a lot, talks a lot, or has different opinions to ours, we don't write them off. We become more accepting because we've discovered that's the only way to enjoy people. With those who are very different from us, we choose to be fascinated rather than disgusted!

NO ONE'S PERFECT

Several years back, I had a secretary, Tereska. She was intelligent, helpful, friendly, caring, hardworking and always arrived ten minutes late for work. I said to her often, "Tereska, it is important that someone is in the office from nine o'clock. Will you make a point of being here at nine?" She would say, "Yes", and arrive next day at ten past!

I began to let this problem worry me. I would say to myself, "Why does she do this to me?" I dwelled on her lateness. I lost my perspective. I lost sight of the fact that she was a wonderful secretary, and I concentrated on the one thing I didn't like.

Finally one day I looked at my own behavior. I realized that I was getting to the office by nine just to be there when she came late – so that I could make the most of being irritated. When she arrived, I would shake my head and say to myself, "I don't believe this!" And I noticed something else about me – I secretly enjoyed being irritated. If it was nine o'clock, and I heard a car door outside, I would be hoping it wasn't Tereska so that I could stay aggravated. That is trivial behavior and I'm a little embarrassed to recall it, but I don't think I'm alone.

I had a capable and loyal assistant, yet I managed to concentrate on her one shortcoming.

How often do we focus on people's faults instead of their attributes? How often do we complain, when if we're really honest with ourselves, we're enjoying the complaining . . . ?

We sit in front of the TV knowing that Uncle Fred is going to come in and turn up the volume – we're just waiting for it – and we're already getting ready to be irritated about it. Fred arrives and turns up the volume, and we say to ourselves "I HATE it when he does that", but inside we're secretly hoping he'll do it anyway.

I have a theory that if we let something worry us, people keep doing it to us. If your husband makes big noises when he eats, and you hate it, and you start waiting for those noises, he'll never let you down. If your son leaves doors open, and you hate it, and you sit there waiting for him to do it, he'll make a hobby of it.

When we are irritated by other people, there are two questions we might ask ourselves –

"Why don't I focus on their good points?"

"What am I gaining by being irritated?"

We get irritated mostly because we want to be irritated. For every behavior, there is a "payoff". The payoff in being irritated is that a) we get to be martyrs (I'M OK YOU'RE NOT), and b) we get to blame others (I'M NOT HAPPY AND IT'S YOUR FAULT).

The alternative to being terminally annoyed is to be FLEXIBLE. Bend a little and understand that everyone is different. People have different temperaments, different priorities. Some people shout and scream, and others never get excited, some show every emotion and others never open up, some are always late, some hoard their money and some spend it. Give them some space to be what they are. For the most part, respect others enough to allow them to experience life in their own way. BEND A LITTLE.

Being upset is OK, but it gets in the way of enjoying life. You can, if you choose, decide not to be upset. YOU DON"T PRACTICE TOLERANCE TO BE HOLIER. YOU DO IT TO BE HAPPIER!

IN A NUTSHELL

Life is all about people. If we put too many conditions on how others should behave, we risk cutting ourselves off from life itself.

No doubt you have acquaintances who are less punctual, more thrifty, or less reliable than you, people who drink more or smoke less than you, people who are more talkative, less modest, much sillier or more serious than you are. BE FLEXIBLE. Delight in the differences in those who make up your world. Enjoy them for their uniqueness and you do yourself the most enormous favor.

FROM ME TO YOU

In Making Friends I have followed some major themes — "take responsibility for your own life ... practice tolerance — for everyone's benefit ... emphasize the positive ... to get respect you have to give it ..."

We must be contributors rather than takers — if we want friends, we have to ADD to people's lives. After all, isn't that where the real joy is? .. in helping out, in surprising people, in doing that little extra ... sometimes it's simply "being there."

We must have fun and be fun.

Others also want us to be real. To be a friend we don't need to become more complicated or sophisticated. Rather we peel off a few layers and reveal something of ourselves.

There can be no last word on making friends. Daily, people will confound, confuse, frustrate and delight us, and we can never expect totally to figure them out. There are no formulas for friendship, but there are some rough paths we can follow.

May you find some benefit from the thoughts in this little book, and may you gather more than your share of joy, laughter and lasting friendships along your path.

Acknowledgements

THANK YOU TO ...

Norma Miraflor, my editor, for knowing just how to transform a manuscript into a book. Your help and knowledge made a world of difference.

To Ian Ward of Media Masters. Your boundless energy and enthusiasm as a publisher are inspirations. Ian, you are really something else!

To Julie, my best friend. Thank you for the love and joy that you bring to my life each day.